BARBARIANS AT BLOOMSBURY
How the British Museum
Appropriated Antiquities

O. M. Lewis

Published by High Tile Books Ltd, 2019

www.hightilebooks.com

A CIP catalogue record for this book is available from the British Library

ISBN: 978-0-9954953-6-4

Cover design by Averill Buchanan

Text design and typesetting by Averill Buchanan

Printed and bound in Great Britain by Clays Ltd, Elcograf S.p.A

MIX
Paper from
responsible sources
FSC
www.fsc.org
FSC® C018072

In memory of Dr James T. Clarke and Stephen N. Lunn

CONTENTS

PART III

ACKNOWLEDGEMENTS

I would like to thank:

Lucy Aliband for her invaluable contribution in converting mountains of evidence, relating to the taking of antiquities from a myriad of ancient sites, into a coherent narrative.

Averill Buchanan for editing, proofreading, typesetting and indexing the book, and for designing the cover. This is the fifth book Averill has done for me in four years.

Stephen Brough for his comments and assistance.

Alice Lewis for researching at the British Library and for her comments on the manuscript.

Stephen W. Garbutt for his comments on the manuscript.

Stephen Lewis and Daria Prigioni for their encouragement.

Dr James T. Clarke and Stephen N. Lunn, school friends to whose memory this book is dedicated, for their shared enthusiasm during this long-term project.

ABBREVIATIONS

ADM	Admiralty
BM	British Museum
CO	Colonial Office
FO	Foreign Office
HC	House of Commons
T	Treasury
TNA	The National Archives
UK PP	United Kingdom Parliamentary Papers
WO	War Office

PART I

CHAPTER 1

Antiquities Taken to Order

There are widely held misconceptions relating to how Assyrian and Babylonian sculptures and Greek and Roman antiquities come to be in the British Museum. The first is that they were collected by adventurous archaeologists, explorers and extraordinary individuals. The second is that these individuals acted unaided and on their own. The third, that the individuals donated everything they found to the British Museum.

This book establishes that none of the foregoing is true.

The fiction of the solitary archaeologist and explorer began in 1870 with the publication of the first history of the formation of the British Museum collections.[1] The myth has its origin in chapters titled 'A Group of Classical Archaeologists and Explorers' and 'Another Group of Archaeologists and Explorers'.

Although some individuals did make valuable contributions to the museum collections, it is erroneous to believe that antiquities were collected by solitary enterprising individuals.

This book explains in detail exactly how antiquities ended up in the British Museum in Bloomsbury. This is the first account to expose the web of deceit spun to conceal the truth about how antiquities come to be there. After a decade of research the story can be told in ten plain words:

> The trustees of the British Museum took whatever they fancied.

---

[1] Edward Edwards, *Lives of The Founders of the British Museum; with notices of its chief augmentors and other benefactors 1570–1870* (London: Trübner and Co., 1870).

This book is concerned with objects in the British Museum collections that satisfy two criteria: first, they are Assyrian and Babylonian sculptures and/or Greek and Roman antiquities; second, they were taken under the specific directions of the trustees. This book is not concerned, therefore, with antiquities or other objects that were either purchased by the museum in the open market or donated to the museum. For example, the Parthenon Sculptures (known as the Elgin Marbles) were purchased by the museum with a grant voted by parliament. They were not taken under *the specific directions of the trustees*; therefore, they are outside the scope of this book. How the British Museum obtained the Parthenon Sculptures is explained in *The Mortgage on the Elgin Marbles*.[2]

* * *

The trustees took the antiquities they coveted to order. The way they did this was covered up in elaborate and effective ways. The cover-up continues to this day, with the result that it is universally believed that the trustees have clean hands with regard to the formation of the antiquities collection. They do not.

In 1874, the Keeper of Greek and Roman Antiquities at the museum candidly explained how the collection was formed. He was blunt about the role of both the trustees and the government:

> It has been acquired by purchase, by donations, and also through the exploration of ancient sites, *conducted by the Government, by the trustees*, or by private enterprise. [emphasis added][3]

The fiction of the adventurous archaeologists, explorers and extraordinary individuals was created to remove any sign that the British government and the trustees had played a role in excavations. This was done for three reasons. Firstly, there was no permission to excavate and take antiquities. Secondly, there was permission but the antiquities taken were beyond the scope and extent of the permission granted. Thirdly, there was permission but it is now embarrassing to admit to the destruction of important cultural sites by removing tons of antiquities.

---

[2] O.M. Lewis, *The Mortgage on the Elgin Marbles* (London: High Tile Books, 2016).
[3] C. T. Newton, ed., *The Collection of Ancient Greek Inscriptions in the British Museum* (Oxford: Clarendon Press, 1874), Preface, n.p.

How did the trustees of the British Museum (at meetings in London in the mid to late 1800s) possibly identify antiquities to be taken to order? They pinpointed them from descriptions, drawings and photographs, and then sent individuals to take what they wanted. In particular:

- they studied descriptions and architectural drawings made by early explorers. For example, they used drawings made by the Society of Dilettanti at Priene (south-west Turkey) in 1764 to take *eighty tons of marble* from there in 1869. A second example relates to a marble statue described in 1821 by Captain Frederick Beechey (Royal Navy) as a 'large torso in armour' in Cyrene (North Africa). Forty years later, in 1860, this very statue was taken by a Royal Engineer on an expedition conducted by the trustees (see Chapter 13);

- they studied sketches and drawings made by explorers of the day and then employed those same explorers to return to the sites they had discovered to point out (to Royal Engineers and crews of HM Ships) what the trustees wanted. For example, Charles Fellows, who discovered Xanthus in south-west Turkey, was engaged by the trustees to return there and point out where to find what the trustees wanted (see Chapter 15);

- they sent artists, employed by the museum, to excavations and then used their drawings to cherry-pick what to take. This entailed sawing marble and stone to take artefacts and inscriptions. For example, the trustees appointed three successive artists in Assyria whose drawings directly led to the removal, by Henry Rawlinson, of objects which he claimed were 'obtained by me according to *the wishes of the trustees*' [emphasis added][4] (see Chapter 10); and

- they used photographs to identify what to take. For example, in 1859 a keeper at the British Museum wrote that a Royal Engineer took 'upwards of 300 photographic negatives containing views of sculptures, excavations and scenery at Bodrum [Halicarnassus],

---

[4] Letter from Sir Henry Rawlinson to the Principal Librarian, British Museum, 2 April 1856. UK PP, 1857–8 (379), p. 14.

Cnidus and Branchidae.'[5] With these photographs the trustees could *dictate* what to put in the majority of the 385 cases transported in the three shipments referred to in Chapter 4.

Therefore, it was not difficult for the trustees to point to the antiquities they fancied.

Archaeologists and explorers did not use their own resources to take antiquities. They were funded by the British government. Furthermore, they were assisted by the Foreign Office, the Treasury, the Admiralty and the War Office, which supplied stores and Royal Engineer sappers to excavate. The list of stores issued for the expedition to Bodrum in 1866 included 'pick axes 200, chisels 100'. The list has eighty-nine lines containing over 2,000 items.[6] The Foreign Office instructed the Admiralty to make an HM Ship available to the expedition and said that its crew 'should consist of about 160 men'.[7] The Admiralty was ordered to transport antiquities for the British Museum and to dig for the museum too.

Many of the archaeologists were employees of the British Museum. Some archaeologists were appointed as British consuls in order to facilitate the taking of antiquities. As consuls they were paid salaries by the Foreign Office. Some of the individuals were in the military, clearly employed by the government.

The fact that archaeologists and explorers were employees and agents of the British Museum and/or the British government is important. This explains how all the antiquities they found were transported, by the Admiralty, *directly* to the British Museum's door. None of the explorers and archaeologists sold anything to the museum because, as employees and agents, the antiquities were not their property to sell.

The trustees made practical use of drawings to secure government grants to take antiquities. In 1846, the museum applied to the Treasury for funding to conduct excavations in Assyria. To entice the Treasury, the museum enclosed

[5] 'Mr. Newton's Discoveries in Asia Minor', *The Times*, 5 September 1859, p. 9.
[6] Letter from War Department to E. Hammond (Treasury), 27 October 1856. TNA, FO 78/1334, pp.115–17.
[7] Letter from Earl of Clarendon to Admiralty, 22 September 1856. TNA, FO 78/1334, pp. 51–2.

> extracts from the correspondence of Mr. Layard, and
> rough tracings from his drawings of some of the objects
> discovered. These documents will suffice to prove to
> your Lordships that the trustees do not exaggerate the
> importance of the proposed acquisition.[8]

The drawings helped secure Treasury funding in 1846.
Thereafter, the Treasury funded British Museum excavations
in Assyria for three decades (see Chapter 10 and Appendix
1). With the full support and backing of the government, the
trustees could take what they wanted.

Part II of this book explains how antiquities were taken from
those 'ancient sites' at which the explorations were '*conducted by
the Government, by the trustees*'.

---

[8] Letter from J. Forshall to the Treasury, 22 July 1846, *Report of Select Committee on
Miscellaneous Expenditure.* UK PP, 1847–48 (543), p. 214.

CHAPTER 2

Aggressive Procurement

> The Trustees ... are desirous to secure the aid of H. M.
> Government in enlarging the Collections by every means
> in its power and more particularly through the Officers
> of the Navy and Army serving on foreign stations and
> other persons administering the affairs of our colonial
> dependencies.

This petition was made by Reverend Josiah Forshall, Principal
Librarian of the British Museum, in a letter to Edward Hawkins,
Keeper at the Museum, and dated 15 April 1836.[1]

In 1857, the Admiralty, under the directions of the Foreign
Office, delivered to the British Museum 218 cases containing
parts of one of the Seven Wonders of the Ancient World:
the Mausoleum of Halicarnassus. The trustees thanked the
Foreign Secretary, hailing it as *'fresh proof* of His Lordship's
desire to promote the interests of the institution' [emphasis
added].[2] 'His Lordship' was the Earl of Clarendon, the Foreign
Secretary.

After the Admiralty delivered a further 110 cases containing,
in the main, more of the Mausoleum of Halicarnassus, the British
Museum thanked the Earl of Malmesbury (who succeeded
Clarendon as Foreign Secretary) and expressed

> the deep sense that the trustees entertain of the liberality
> of Her Majesty's Government in the proceedings taken

---

[1] David. M. Wilson, *The British Museum: A History* (London: British Museum Press,
2002), p. 102.
[2] Letter from A Panizzi to E .Hammond, 22 July 1857. TNA, FO 781/1335, pp. 25–6.

> to secure these valuable monuments of ancient art for
> the National Collections.[3]

Clarendon and Malmesbury, the Foreign Secretaries, were both trustees of the British Museum.

The museum's request for government assistance to expand the collections 'by every means in its power' led to a period of aggressive procurement. The trustees took Assyrian and Babylonian sculptures and Greek and Roman antiquities in prodigious quantities between 1839 and 1900.

At a time when Britain ruled the waves and much of the world, the trustees asked the government to help expand the collections. A former director of the museum claimed it was not long after the request that expeditions were being planned 'to bring home prestigious antiquities to London'.[4] The British government embraced the museum's request.

Their first step was to put the museum in a privileged position by removing Custom House duty on the import of antiquities destined for the museum.[5]

Secondly, the government funded individuals to take antiquities for the museum. Specific grants to take antiquities from named sites are entered in British Museum Accounts presented to parliament (available online) and in Treasury records (at The National Archives). The funding to take antiquities went through public accounts; it was not done covertly (with the exception of antiquities taken from Priene, covered in Chapter 9, and Carthage, discussed in Chapter 14). Funding British Museum excavations was done openly, but today this is covered up, due in part, no doubt, to embarrassment.

The individuals funded by the British government to take antiquities for the British Museum included employees of the museum (see Chapters 9 and 18); British consuls (see Chapters 7, 12, 16, 19 and 20); Army and Navy officers (see Chapter 13); and arbitrary individuals (see Chapters 11 and 15).

---

[3] Letter from A. Panizzi to Earl of Malmesbury, 20 January 1859. TNA, FO 78/1490, p. 256.

[4] Wilson, *The British Museum*, p.102.

[5] Lucia Patrizio Gunning, *The British Consular Service in the Aegean and the Collection of Antiquities for the British Museum* (Farnham: Ashgate, 2009), p. 153n35; 15 March 1838, British Museum Archive, Letter Book n.48, fols 14–15.

The third way the government assisted was by arranging for *all* the antiquities taken by the individuals to be transported to England by the Admiralty in HM Ships at the government's expense.

The activities of government-funded individuals led to the British Museum having one of the most comprehensive and outstanding collections of antiquities in the world. But their activities led to widespread and deliberate mutilation and destruction of cultural heritage and important archaeological sites. The damage to cultural heritage is incalculable. The remains of some of the sites devastated under the direction of the trustees of the British Museum are today UNESCO World Heritage Sites.

* * *

In 1992, Ian Jenkins, Curator at the British Museum, wrote a book which he claimed presented a 'detailed account' of the acquisition of the British Museum's sculpture collections.[6] Jenkins wrote that the antiquities in the British Museum, unlike those at the Louvre, were not gathered out of an urge for national self-aggrandisement. He maintained the sculpture collection was formed 'through a series of remarkable accidents'.[7] However, the museum's request for government aid in enlarging the collections by every means in its power *is* self-aggrandisement.

Following the museum's request, antiquities were taken, in bulk, under the *specific* directions of the trustees and with government funding. There was nothing accidental about the way in which the antiquities were collected.

Jenkins maintained that the composition of the museum sculpture collection reflected 'the enterprise of a few extraordinary individuals'. He singled out Charles Fellows at Lycia; Austen Layard in Assyria; Charles Newton at Halicarnassus, Didyma and Cnidus; Robert Murdoch Smith and E. A. Porcher at Cyrene; Richard Pullan at Priene; John Turtle Wood at Ephesus and Nathan Davis at Carthage.[8]

---

[6] Ian Jenkins, *Archaeologists & Aesthetes in the Sculpture Galleries of the British Museum 1800–1939* (London: British Museum Press, 1992), p. 9.

[7] Jenkins, *Archaeologists & Aesthetes*, p. 13.

[8] Jenkins, *Archaeologists & Aesthetes*, pp.13–14 & 175–6.

Jenkins covers the activities of the some of these individuals in depth, but others not at all. For example, John Turtle Wood gets a single sentence, but it is not in connection with Ephesus; it relates to the museum's lack of space for what Wood collected from there. Smith and Porcher at Cyrene get two sentences, and Pullan at Priene gets a single sentence.[9]

In this book, every one of the named 'extraordinary individuals' gets a dedicated chapter explaining what they took, how they were funded and how the antiquities were transported to the British Museum.

None of the above 'extraordinary individuals' sold a single object to the British Museum. All acquisitions made by the museum were listed in British Museum Accounts (available via UK Parliamentary Papers online).

While none of them sold a thing, *all of the antiquities* they discovered are in the museum collections. This is because every one of these individuals was either an employee or an agent of the British Museum and/or the British government.

The enterprise of 'extraordinary individuals' and others is exposed in this book as never before. The myth of the solitary and enterprising explorers and archaeologists will be shattered.

---

[9] Jenkins, *Archaeologists & Aesthetes*, p. 212.

CHAPTER 3

Tons of Antiquities

Museums acquire antiquities in all manner of ways, but how does a museum procure tons of antiquities from a single site? The British Museum and government took tons of antiquities from single sites. There are important differences between obtaining single objects versus tons of antiquities. Removing tons entails the physical destruction of sites. Tons is not used here as a figure of speech.

The Admiralty, using HM Ships, transported the following for the British Museum:

- 80 tons of marble (in 110 cases) from the Temple of Athena Polias at Priene (Chapter 9);
- 80 tons of marble (in 82 cases) from Xanthus (Chapter 15);
- over 60 tons of marble (in excess of 100 cases) from the Temple of Diana at Ephesus, also known as the Temple of Artemis (Chapter 11);
- over 100 tons (in about 500 cases) from Assyria and Babylon (Chapter 10);
- 385 cases and 160 blocks of marble from Halicarnassus, Cnidus and Branchidae (Chapter 8);
- 103 cases from Cyrene in North Africa (Chapter 13);
- 93 cases from Carthage (Chapter 14); and
- significant quantities of antiquities from Rhodes, Sicily, Crete and Cyprus (Chapters 12, 16, 17 and 18).

The number of cases and tonnages are from unimpeachable Admiralty and Treasury primary sources held at The National Archives.

The sources do not always cite both the number of cases and tonnage, but do cite one or the other. There are no guidelines as to the size of the cases. One case contained the Lion from Cnidus, housed today in the British Museum's covered Great Court, which weighed an estimated ten tons (see Chapter 4).

The following were the contents of one case transported by HMS *Gorgon* from Bodrum: 'Part of Draped Figure, piece of Cornice, pieces of lion, pieces of Frieze, Mausoleum (case no. 73)'. Clearly these objects would not fit in a small case. One case of antiquities is the centrepiece of the engraving *Arrival of the Remains of the Tomb of Mausolus at the British Museum.*[1] The engraving depicts six men hauling a large wooden case up a ramp on the steps in the British Museum's front courtyard. It can be assumed, however, given that HM Ships transported over one hundred cases at a time, that the majority of the cases would be of standard size to maximise storage space in the ship's hold.

Therefore, there was no series of remarkable accidents. This was state appropriation of 'prestigious antiquities'.

The trustees of the British Museum hoarded antiquities. The quantities taken were so vast they could *never* be put on public display. Tons of antiquities were taken from ancient sites and buried in British Museum stores (see Chapter 22).

According to a former director, by the early 1800s the museum had become proactive in collecting antiquities from the Mediterranean.[2] However, there is a clear distinction between 'collecting' and taking.

Taking is synonymous with theft. It is for the reader to decide, having read the evidence, if the trustees of the British Museum collected or took antiquities.

---

[1] 'The Arrival of the Remains of the Tomb of Mausolus at the British Museum', *The Illustrated London News* 22 January 1859, pp. 83 and 85.

[2] David M. Wilson, *The British Museum: A History* (London: The British Museum Press, 2002), p. 68.

CHAPTER 4

Antiquities Destined 'for British Museum'

The trustees took tons of antiquities from ancient sites with the assistance of the British government, which helped in many ways. One was to transport antiquities for the museum. Chapter 6 names fifty of Her Majesty's Ships that transported antiquities for the British Museum between 1839 and 1891.

The original log books of HM Ships are at The National Archives in London. They name the ports and the dates when the antiquities were loaded and discharged for the British Museum. The following are six sample entries, listed in chronological order, from the log books of HM Ships that transported antiquities specifically '*for British Museum*' (emphasis added):

> 1858 – HMS *Supply*, 20 July 1858 at anchorage at the Ruins of Cnidus (South-West Turkey): 'Stowing away cases *for British Museum* Nos. 291, 292, 294, 296, 286, 287 & 288'.[1]

These cases, in the main, contained parts of one of the Seven Wonders of the Ancient World: the Mausoleum of Halicarnassus. On this voyage, HMS *Supply* transported cases numbered 218 to 329. Case 312 (loaded on 27 August 1858) contained the colossal Lion of Cnidus, today in the British Museum covered Great Court. On a subsequent voyage, *Supply* transported cases numbered 330 to 385. Cases numbered 1 to 217 were

---

[1] TNA, ADM 53/6598.

transported by HMS *Gorgon*. There are published inventories of the contents of the 385 cases.[2]

> 1868 – HMS *Terrible*, 27 March 1868 at Portsmouth: 'Employed hoisting out antiquities *for British Museum*'.[3]

> 1872 – HMS *Agincourt*, 8 May 1872 at Malta: 'Dockyard party returned with cases containing marbles etc. *for British Museum*'.[4] [Marbles in Victorian times meant Greek and Roman marble statues and sculptures.]

> 1874 – HMS *Revenge*, 11 February 1874 at Malta: 'Employed hoisting in marble blocks *for British Museum*'.[5]

> 1881 – HMS *Hecla*, 12 September 1881, at anchor off Alexandretta: 'Received monolith from the shore for conveyance to Malta *for British Museum*.'

> 1891 – HMS *Amphion*, 10 February 1891 at Alexandria: 'Hoisted on the stone winged bull property *of the British Museum*'.[6]

In excess of 1,300 cases of antiquities were transported to England over sixty years (1839–1891). On every single voyage, the captains of HM Ships *knew* that the antiquities they were transporting to England belonged to the British Museum. The fact that this was known onboard ships, even before the antiquities reached Britain's shores, establishes that the antiquities were not found and transported to England by individuals.

The original log books of HM Ships form part of the mountain of evidence that explodes the myth relating to the supposed contributions of extraordinary individuals.

[2] *Papers respecting the Excavations at Budrum: Presented to both Houses of Parliament by Command of Her Majesty* (London: Harrison and Sons, 1858), UK PP, 1857–58 [2359][2378], pp. 24–27; *Further Papers respecting the Excavations at Budrum and Cnidus: Presented to the House of Lords by Command of Her Majesty.* 1859 (London: Harrison and Sons, 1859), UK PP 1859 Series 2 [2575] pp. 35–8; pp. 95–101; and 'List of Cases shipped in Her Majesty's ship Gorgon', Treasury Register of Papers. Public Offices A–M 1857. British Museum. TNA, T 2/238, enclosure No. 11, p. 24.
[3] TNA, ADM 53/9346.
[4] TNA, ADM 53/10401.
[5] TNA, ADM 53/1084.
[6] TNA, ADM 53/12454.

CHAPTER 5

The Trustees of the British Museum

In the mid-1800s it would have been impossible to assemble in Britain a more powerful and influential group than the trustees of the British Museum. The following were automatically trustees by virtue of the office and position:

> The Archbishop of Canterbury; the Lord Chancellor; Speaker of the House of Commons; Lord President of the Council; First Lord of the Treasury [the prime minister]; Lord Privy Seal; First Lord of the Admiralty; Lord Steward; Lord Chamberlain; all the Principal Secretaries of State; Bishop of London; Chancellor of the Exchequer; Lord Chief Justice, Queen's Bench; Master of the Rolls; Lord Chief Justice, Common Pleas; Attorney-General; Solicitor-General; President of the Royal Society; President of the College of Physicians; President of the Society of Antiquaries; and President of the Royal Academy.[1]

In addition, the monarch had the right to appoint one trustee, known as the Royal Trustee. Further, among the small group of elected trustees one was always a member of parliament, appointed specifically to represent the interests of the museum in the House of Commons. There were six trustees who inherited a trusteeship, known as Family Trustees. One family was the Elgins. The 7th Lord Elgin (and his successors) was made a trustee of the British Museum by an Act of Parliament when he sold the Elgin Marbles to the British Museum in 1816.[2]

---

[1] *The British Imperial Calendar* (London: Varnham & Co, 1860), pp. 242–4.
[2] *An Act to vest the Elgin Collection of ancient Marbles and Sculpture in the Trustees of the British Museum for the Use of the Public 1816*, Section 4.

This right subsisted until the British Museum Act 1963 altered the composition of trustees.

In 1973, when museums were actively seeking wealthy trustees, a journalist asked a trustee of the Museum of Modern Art, New York, what they looked for in a new trustee. He replied, 'Money'. 'Is that all,' asked the journalist? The trustee said they looked for three things, 'Money, money, money.'[3]

If Antonio Panizzi (Principal Librarian of the British Museum, 1856–1866) had been asked the same question, he would have replied that he looked for power and influence, but he would have added that his trustees had all the power needed to expand the museum collections at will.

In 1880, after decades of aggressive procurement by the museum, it was asserted that:

> In the case of the British Museum, the Treasury seems to have been the chief governing power, and the Prime Minister of the day and the Chancellor of the Exchequer the authorities who have been in direct communication with the trustees.[4]

The line between the government and the trustees was blurred when it came to taking antiquities for the British Museum.

All the trustees were kept fully informed on the expansion of the collections; in particular, they were kept advised of the Admiralty's activities on behalf of the museum. This included being notified of the names of HM Ships that transported antiquities. The following are three examples:

- a letter from the Admiralty advising that HMS *Terrible* was ordered to Smyrna to bring home antiquities for the British Museum from Ephesus was tabled at a meeting of the trustees;[5]
- a letter from the Admiralty relating to sixty-three cases of antiquities transported from Cyrene on HMS *Melpomene* was tabled at a meeting of the trustees;[6] and

---

[3] Karl E. Meyer, *The Plundered Past: The Traffic in Art Treasures* (London: Penguin, 1973), p. 58.

[4] 'The British Museum and its Trustees', *Aberdeen Weekly Journal*, 23 August 1880, Issue 7962.

[5] Correspondence and papers, letter dated 29 November 1867. TNA, ADM 1/6028.

[6] Correspondence and papers, letter dated 28 December 1861. TNA, ADM 1/5777.

- the Admiralty recorded the discovery of the torso of a colossal figure at Elea (the port of Pergamos), adding, 'The attention of the Trustees of the British Museum should be called with a view to the removal.'[7]

At meetings with the prime minister, occasionally chaired by the Archbishop of Canterbury, the trustees sanctioned, approved and instigated the excavations at the ancient sites discussed in Part II of this book.

---

[7] Admiralty Digest 1860, Case 90a British Museum. TNA, ADM 12/689.

CHAPTER 6

The British Museum and the Admiralty

There is no tribute to the Admiralty in the British Museum. There should be. The Admiralty played a pivotal role in making the British Museum one of the greatest museums in the world.

The museum was founded in 1753. Histories of the museum describe the ancient sites where antiquities were found, but none explains, in any detail, how antiquities were transported to the museum.

Britain is an island; therefore, Assyrian and Babylonian sculptures and Greek and Roman antiquities had to be transported by sea (with the exception of those from Roman Britain). In the grand scheme of things, how antiquities were transported to England would be of little significance, save for one fact: the Assyrian and Babylonian sculptures and Greek and Roman antiquities taken under the directions of the trustees were all transported by the Admiralty in HM Ships or, on occasion, merchant ships chartered by the Admiralty.

HM Ships transported antiquities for the British Museum taken from (in alphabetical order) Alexandria, Athens, Branchidae, Carthage, Cnidus, Crete, Cyprus, Cyrene, Elea, Ephesus, Halicarnassus, Kalymna, Kaos, Khorsabad, Kos, Kuyunjik, Mytilene, Nimroud, Nineveh, Petra, Priene, Rhodes, Sicily, Smyrna, Thasos and Xanthus.

Clearly the Admiralty did not come to transport antiquities to England following 'a series of remarkable accidents' as claimed by Jenkins. The fact that the Admiralty transported *all* the antiquities is the single most important factor in unravelling how the trustees of the British Museum took antiquities.

19

The Foreign Office, the Treasury and the Admiralty worked hand in glove on behalf of the British Museum. Therefore, any account that explains how antiquities come to be in the British Museum cannot be written without explaining the role of the Admiralty. This will become apparent in Part II of this book, which explains how and what was taken from specific ancient sites.

The Admiralty did not transport the antiquities because there was no other available shipping capacity. There was a superabundance of ships. Malta was a transshipment hub for antiquities. *The Malta Times* (established 1840) recorded the *daily* arrival and departures of P&O Company mail ships (established 1837), Royal Mail ships, British merchant ships and foreign merchant ships. All were available to transport antiquities, but none did.

There are two reasons why the Admiralty transported *all* antiquities. Firstly, when antiquities were taken under the direction of the trustees, the Foreign Office instructed the Admiralty to transport the antiquities. Secondly, whenever antiquities were taken by the trustees, the Treasury paid all procurement costs, including transportation costs. Further, HM Ships could be ordered to go anywhere at any time. In 1857, HMS *Supply* was ordered to make a round trip from Bodrum to Smyrna to pick up a marble statue:

> Requested by the Trustees of the British Museum to purchase a valuable statue at Smyrna ... I proceeded to that place in HMS Supply ... after taking on board the statue returned to Bodrum.[1]

It would have been impractical for the trustees to use anything but an HM Ship.

Therefore, when the Admiralty incurred expenditure on behalf of the British Museum, it was charged to the Foreign Office who applied to the Treasury. The following is an example of a letter from the Treasury to the Foreign Office in respect of the expedition that is the subject of Chapter 8:

> The Paymaster General has been directed to transfer to the account of Naval Services the sum of £644.14.5 being

---

[1] Letter from C. T. Newton to Earl of Clarendon, 9 December 1857. TNA, FO 78/1335, p. 260, and ADM 53/6598.

the amount of supplies issued by the Naval Department to the Bodrum Expedition from 1857 to 1859, also to the Account of Army Services the sum of £771.11.8, being the amount of stores supplied by the War Department to that Expedition.[2]

When antiquities were packed and ready to be transported to England, the trustees advised the Foreign Office, or, on occasion, the Treasury, depending on expenses to be incurred, which, in turn, directed the Admiralty to transport them. The following fifty HM Ships transported antiquities for the British Museum between 1839–1891:

HMS *Acheron*
HMS *Agincourt*
HMS *Algiers*
HMS *Amphion*
HMS *Antelope*
HMS *Apollo*
HMS *Assurance*
HMS *Belvidera*
HMS *Caledonia*
HMS *Cambridge*
HMS *Caradoc*
HMS *Chanticleer*
HMS *Condor*
HMS *Curacoa*
HMS *Fantome*
HMS *Foxhound*
HMS *Gorgon*
HMS *Hecla*
HMS *Himalaya*
HMS *Humber*
HMS *Industry*
HMS *Jumna*
HMS *Kertch*
HMS *Lord Warden*
HMS *Medea*
HMS *Medina*
HMS *Meeanee*

---

[2] Treasury Out-Letters to Foreign Office 1860–1863. TNA, T 12/2, p. 28.

HMS *Megaera*
HMS *Melita*
HMS *Melpomene*
HMS *Monarch*
HMS *Orontes*
HMS *Pelican*
HMS *Perseverance*
HMS *Phoebe*
HMS *Rapid*
HMS *Revenge*
HMS *Scourge*
HMS *Simoon*
HMS *Siren*
HMS *Supply*
HMS *Swiftsure*
HMS *Sylvia*
HMS *Talavera*
HMS *Tamar*
HMS *Terrible*
HMS *Tyne*
HMS *Vesuvius*
HMS *Warspite*
HMS *Wizard*

Some of the ships transported antiquities more than once. The record for the most journeys with antiquities is held by HMS *Supply*, which made seven. In addition to these ships, the Admiralty chartered merchant ships if an HM Ship was unavailable. These included *Christiana Carnel*, *Manuel*, *W.S. Lindsay* and *Firefly*. Appendix 2 contains a chronological list of HM Ships, what they transported and from where, in each case citing primary sources at The National Archives.

The British Museum knew precisely which HM Ships were available to transport antiquities. This is because the Admiralty sent the museum copies of the quarterly *Navy List*. It named all ships in the Royal Navy, specified where the ship was stationed, and named the captains and officers.[3] The trustees made good use of the *Navy List*.

---

[3] *The Navy List* (London: John Murray, 1839–91).

The museum was demanding when it came to transporting antiquities. For example, it protested when 135 cases of antiquities failed to arrive in England from Malta on board HMS *Serapis* and HMS *Crocodile* as anticipated,[4] and insisted that the 135 cases were to be transported at the first opportunity. Panizzi's assistant wrote to the Admiralty to say that he had been informed that HMS *Himalaya* and HMS *Simoon* would shortly be leaving Malta for England and *demanded* these ships transport the cases to England.[5]

The Admiralty transported prodigious loads for the British Museum. In 1870, eighty tons of marble were transported from Smyrna in a single shipment (see Chapter 9). However, the Admiralty sometimes declined the museum's requests, usually because the loads were either too small or too heavy. The following are examples.

In 1856, the Admiralty dismissed a request from the museum to transport five tons: the 'Collection being so small [the Admiralty] Board considers that it would be better to send it home in a merchant vessel.'[6]

The Admiralty dismissed a load from Egypt as being too heavy. Yet the Admiralty had transported parts of the Mausoleum of Halicarnassus and Cleopatra's Needle from Egypt, now installed on the Embankment in London. It is difficult to imagine what the load was from Egypt that was too heavy – a pyramid?

In 1869, the Treasury issued a general direction to Customs and Excise: all antiquities for the British Museum were to be treated the same as bullion for the Bank of England; the cases were not to be inspected when they landed.[7]

The Admiralty's immense contribution to the British Museum was not limited to transporting antiquities. At some sites, Navy marines excavated on behalf of the museum (see Chapters 11 and 14). This was one of the direct consequences of the museum having secured government aid 'in enlarging the Collections ... through the Officers of the Navy'.[8]

---

[4] Admiralty Correspondence 1869. British Museum. TNA, ADM 1/6139.

[5] Admiralty Correspondence 1869. British Museum. TNA, ADM 1/6139.

[6] Admiralty Digest 1856, Case 90a British Museum. TNA, ADM 12/624.

[7] Books of Out-Letters to Customs and Excise 1867–1870. TNA, T 11/116, p. 334.

[8] Wilson, *The British Museum: A History*, p. 102.

The following example highlights the extent to which the Admiralty assisted the museum. In 1858, two sarcophagi of white marble were discovered in Crete by Captain Spratt of HMS *Medina*. One weighed '7½ tons and the other about 4 tons.'[9] Spratt had photographic apparatus onboard ship (see Chapter 23). The Admiralty forwarded Spratt's photographs to the trustees who instructed Spratt to buy the sarcophagi for £100. The trustees were obliged to raise their offer to £150.[10] Payment was made by the paymaster of HMS *Medina*.[11] The two sarcophagi entered the museum collections in 1862.[12] Therefore, Captain Spratt found, photographed, negotiated, paid for, and transported the sarcophagi to England. 'Captain Spratt of *Medina* thanked by Trustees of Museum', the Admiralty recorded.[13]

This establishes that the Admiralty kept meticulous records of captains' activities. This is significant because, with the exception of Captain Spratt paying for the sarcophagi, there is no record of *any* captain or paymaster of any of the fifty HM Ships listed having paid for *anything* transported by the HM Ships. It would appear, from Admiralty and Treasury records, that tons of antiquities were taken for the British Museum without payment.

If payments had been made for antiquities, the payments would be recorded in at least two places. The first, in the British Museum ledger in the Treasury Register of Papers (T2 series at The National Archives). Whenever parliament granted monies to the museum for an acquisition, the Treasury entered the amount as a credit in the museum account. For example in 1855, '£3,981 for purchases at the sale of the Bernal Collection'.[14] The second place payments were recorded was in the British Museum's own accounts.

The Treasury recorded all amounts spent on excavations and transportation of antiquities, but nothing for purchasing antiquities.

---

[9] 'Naval and Military Intelligence', *The Times*, 17 January 1861, p. 12.

[10] Index K–O 1860, HMS *Medina*, 'Failure of negotiations Sarcophagi'. TNA, ADM 12/678.

[11] Admiralty Digest 1860, Case 90a British Museum. TNA, ADM 12/689.

[12] British Museum Accounts, 31 March 1862. UK PP, 1862 (200), p. 17.

[13] Case 90a British Museum. TNA, ADM 12/736.

[14] Treasury Register of Papers. Public Offices A–M 1855, British Museum. TNA, T 2/230.

* * *

The following is how historians and writers have explained how antiquities ended up in the British Museum.

The first history of the museum, Edwards' *Lives of The Founders of the British Museum*, does not mention the Admiralty or an HM Ship, despite the fact that, when it was published in 1870, the Admiralty had been transporting antiquities for the museum for over three decades (see Appendix 2).

The most authoritative modern history of the museum, written by David M. Wilson and published in 2002, names five HM Ships. Only two of the five are in the above list of fifty HM Ships: HMS *Gorgon* that transported antiquities from Bodrum, and HMS *Supply* that transported antiquities including the colossal Lion of Cnidus.[15] The other three ships are HMS *Colossus*, which sank in 1798 with part of the Hamilton Collection,[16] HMS *Herald* that transported 'Fijian material',[17] and HMS *Topaze*, which transported the stone statues from Easter Island.[18] HMS *Topaze* is not in the list of fifty HM Ships because the Easter Island statues in the museum were not taken *under directions of the trustees*. Therefore, Wilson's history of the museum does not cover the Admiralty's contribution.

A recent book which claims in its title that it will explain how treasures 'ended up in museums' (which implies transportation) does not name a single one of the fifty HM Ships that transported antiquities for the British Museum.[19] Tiffany Jenkins' book, *Keeping their Marbles: how the treasures of the past ended up in museums...and why they should stay there*, names three HM Ships, *Endeavour*, *Adventure* and *Resolution*, as having transported material that is now in the British Museum collections. But these ships only transported ethnographical material and natural history from the Southern Oceans in the mid to late 1700s, decades before the trustees were proactive in conducting excavations at ancient sites.

---

[15] Wilson, *The British Museum: A History*, p. 125.

[16] Wilson, *The British Museum: A History*, p. 47.

[17] Wilson, *The British Museum: A History*, p. 159.

[18] Wilson, *The British Museum: A History*, p.176.

[19] Tiffany Jenkins, *Keeping their Marbles: how the treasures of the past ended up in museums ... and why they should stay there* (Oxford: Oxford University Press, 2016).

The British Museum collections consist of eight million objects of which, the museum has stated, only *one* per cent is on public display (see Chapter 22). There are ever increasing calls for the restitution of objects in the collections. 'Keeping' (as Tiffany Jenkins' book title puts it) the objects is no solution; the establishment of British Museum satellite museums around the world may be one way around the problem.

British Museum archives and HM Ships

When work on this book began, researchers at The National Archives had their papers searched as they left in an effort to prevent the theft of documents. Nowadays, researchers' papers are also searched before they *enter*. This is because an historian was caught *inserting* material into some of the files; he subsequently published more than one history based on his misinformation. This was not the first time misinformation had been planted in an archive (nor will it be the last). There is good reason to suspect that misinformation has been inserted in British Museum archives relating to HM Ships that transported antiquities.

In 1936, C. J. Gadd, Keeper of the Department of Egyptian and Assyrian Antiquities at the British Museum, wrote that HMS *Grecian* transported Assyrian antiquities to the museum in May 1847.[20] However, HMS *Grecian*'s original log book establishes that between 15 March 1847 and 17 July 1847 she was anchored at Buenos Aires, from where she sailed to Montevideo.[21]

In 1992, Ian Jenkins, relying on British Museum archives, wrote that HMS *Grecian* transported twelve cases of antiquities from Nineveh which arrived in England in May 1847.[22] The claim by Gadd and Jenkins, that HM *Grecian* transported antiquities in 1847, was not an oversight or error. Jenkins cites, in footnotes, material in the museum archives to back him up: 'O.P.' (original papers, letters and original reports); 'O.R.' (officers' reports, the reports of the various officers of the museum to the trustees), and 'C' (minutes of the Standing Committees of the Trustees). No matter what anything in the museum archives may say, *Grecian*'s original log book establishes

---

[20] C. J. Gadd, *The Stones of Assyria* (London: Chatto & Windus, 1936), p. 33.

[21] TNA, ADM 53/2585.

[22] Jenkins, *Archaeologists & Aesthetes*, p. 155.

that she was not in England in May 1847. The reason why someone, before Gadd, fabricated documentary evidence that *Grecian* transported twelve cases from Nineveh was to instil in the public's mind those twelve cases. The truth is that over five hundred cases were taken from Assyria and Babylon (see Chapter 10).

In another example, Gadd claimed that HMS *Queen* transported marbles from Xanthus in south-west Turkey.[23] Jenkins, relying on Gadd and citing material in British Museum archives, claims that the Xanthian Marbles arrived at Portsmouth aboard HMS *Queen*.[24] However, HMS *Queen* did not transport the Xanthian Marbles. This is how the marbles were actually transported: HMS *Medea* and HMS *Warspite* from the Xanthus River to Malta; from Malta to England onboard HMS *Cambridge* and HMS *Vesuvius*. The log books of these four ships record the days and time of day when the 'Xanthus Marbles' were loaded and discharged. HMS *Cambridge*'s log book records *seventy-eight* cases, with the Xanthus Marbles being discharged at Portsmouth over six consecutive days. HMS *Queen* was used to draw attention away from the ships that actually transported the Xanthus Marbles, marbles that were taken by the trustees of the British Museum but subsequently covered up (see Chapter 15).

The conclusion to be drawn from the sources in the British Museum archives, cited by Jenkins, is that someone planted misinformation at some point before Gadd published his book in 1936. In researching *this* book, no reliance has been placed on British Museum archives.

First-hand accounts and HM Ships

First-hand accounts were written by individuals funded by the government to excavate on behalf of the British Museum. These include John Turtle Wood at Ephesus (Chapter 11), Lieutenants R. M. Smith and E. A. Porcher at Cyrene (Chapter 13), and Nathan Davis at Carthage (Chapter 14). In their accounts they record the arrival and departure of HM Ships sent to collect antiquities. First-hand accounts are an important primary source, but not all are comprehensive. Further, Wood's account contains deliberate misrepresentations relating to the

---

[23] Gadd, *The Stones of Assyria*, p. 56.
[24] Jenkins, *Archaeologists & Aesthetes*, p. 145.

HM Ships that transported the antiquities he excavated (see Chapter 11). Therefore, no reliance has been placed on the first-hand accounts in so far as they relate to HM Ships. Nor has any reliance been placed on reports in newspapers relating to the HM Ships that transported antiquities because mistakes were printed and not corrected.

The National Archives and HM Ships
The only reliable documents relating to the HM Ships that transported antiquities for the British Museum are Admiralty sources at The National Archives (see Chapter 23).

A note on the appendices
Appendices 1, 2 and 3 at the end of this book can be read as a single document. By way of illustration, take as an example the Xanthus Marbles. These can be tracked across the three appendices:

- Appendix 1 sets out parliamentary grants in British Museum Accounts to take marbles from Xanthus.
- Appendix 2 names four HM Ships that transported the marbles from Xanthus.
- Appendix 3 points to engravings of the marbles from Xanthus contemporaneously published by *The Illustrated London News*.

Alternatively, items can be tracked the other way round, from the third appendix to the first. Start with, say, Ephesus in *The Illustrated London News* (Appendix 3), then see the six HM Ships that transported in excess of one hundred cases of marble from Ephesus (Appendix 2) and, finally, source the specific grants made to the British Museum to take the marble from Ephesus (Appendix 1). Sixty tons of marble was taken from the Temple of Diana at Ephesus, one of the Seven Wonders of the Ancient World (see Chapter 11).

The combined appendices are a unique resource but it is not complete. In 1869, 110 cases of marble were taken from the Temple of Athena Polias in Priene. The HM Ships that transported the cases are in Appendix 2, but the amount of money spent on taking the cases is not known and therefore is not in Appendix 1. The expenditure should be recorded in T 5/5 (Treasury Out-Letters to the Admiralty 1869) held at The National Archives. But a page in the index (under 'expenditure') has been replaced with a different colour paper in a different hand. It is not subtly done, but it is an effective way of covering up the amount spent on taking marble from Priene. The tampering only serves to reinforce that there was a cover-up (see Chapter 9). *The Illustrated London News* never covered the marble taken from Priene in 1869, but in the following year there were engravings of marbles taken from Priene in *The Graphic*.[25]

---

[25] 'The Priene Exhibition', *The Graphic*, 12 November 1870, p. 468.

PART II

CHAPTER 7

Greek Islands: Charles Newton,
British Vice-Consul

Charles Thomas Newton read Classics at Oxford and joined the British Museum in 1840 aged twenty-four. He had been at the museum for twelve years when, in 1852, the Foreign Office appointed him British Consul at Rhodes and then Vice-Consul at Mytilene on the Greek island of Lesbos (Rhodes and Lesbos were under Turkish control at the time).

In 1859, Newton returned to the British Museum and wrote a book in which he stated in his introduction:

> In receiving this appointment from the Foreign Office [at Mytilene], I was, at the same time *instructed* to use such opportunities as presented themselves for the acquisition of Antiquities for the British Museum [emphasis added].[1]

A reviewer of Newton's book commented, 'In February 1852 our author was appointed to the Vice-Consulship of Mytilene, but with the express understanding that he was permitted to quit his post in search of antiquities for the British Museum, for which purpose a small additional allowance was granted ... At Malta he assisted at the opening of some ancient tombs'.[2]

In 1854, Newton was briefly Vice-Consul on Rhodes where he pursued the British Museum's interests and noted 'the annual allowance of £50 granted to me by the Foreign Office for my

---

[1] C.T. Newton, *Travels and Discoveries in the Levant* (London: Day & Sons, 1865), vol. 1, Introduction, n.p.

[2] 'Newton's Travels and Discoveries in the Levant', *The Times*, 7 November 1865, p. 7.

expenses in travelling on account of the British Museum'.[3] He
goes on to say that on Rhodes he 'opened a number of tombs
of different kinds' and describes *ten* different kinds of tombs.[4]
Newton was not the only British Consul who robbed tombs (see
Chapters 12 and 16).

He spent eight years (aside from a few months in Rome)
taking antiquities for the British Museum:

> During my official residence in Turkey from 1852 to
> 1859 as Vice-Consul of Mytilene I was able to obtain *one*
> *hundred and fifty-eight* inscriptions from the islands of
> Mytilene, Kalymna, Kos, Rhodes, Kaos and from the sites
> of Halicarnassus, Cnidus and Branchidae on the west
> coast of Asia Minor [emphasis added].[5]

In 2019, only one of the inscriptions taken by Newton was on
public display at the museum. Its caption erroneously states:
'Given by C. T. Newton'.[6] Newton obtained it while Consul at
Mytilene with government funding. Neither this inscription nor
the others he took were his to give.

In 1857, Newton explained in a letter to the Earl of Clarendon
(Foreign Secretary and trustee of the British Museum) that he
visited 'the celebrated Temple of Apollo at Branchidae [near
Geronta] ... the remains of the magnificent temple ... so fully
illustrated by the Dilettanti Society in the first volume of their
Ionian Antiquities'.[7] He took 'ninety-four inscriptions from
the Temple of Apollo'[8] (with inscriptions translated in Part II,
Chapter 4 of his book), sawing the ninety-four inscriptions from
marble blocks. Newton utterly destroyed what remained of the
Temple of Apollo and much more.

It is difficult to establish what, if any, permissions Newton
had to do what he did. All of the above was taken from parts

---

[3] Letter from C.T. Newton to Robert Campbell, 23 November 1854. TNA, FO
78/1017, p. 137.

[4] Newton, *Travels and Discoveries in the Levant*, vol. I, pp. 62–3.

[5] C.T. Newton, ed., *The Collection of Ancient Greek Inscriptions in the British Museum*
(Oxford: The Clarendon Press, 1874), Preface, n.p.

[6] Inscribed altar ...' From Mytilene, BM Room 70, photographed 14 February
2019.

[7] Letter from C.T. Newton to the Earl of Clarendon, 31 December 1857. TNA, FO
78/1335, pp. 284–305.

[8] Newton, ed., *The Collection of Ancient Greek Inscriptions in the British Museum.*

of the Ottoman Empire. When excavations were planned, the Foreign Office obtained permissions from the Porte (the Turkish government) through the British Embassy in Constantinople. Newton wrote in *Travels and Discoveries in the Levant* that 'Lord Stratford [ambassador in Constantinople] [had] obtained for me a firman [permission] enabling me to dig in the Hippodrome [at Therapia]'.[9] But ten pages on, Newton casts doubt on this by claiming, 'Before digging in the Hippodrome I had an interview with Fund Pasha in order *to obtain* the necessary permission' [emphasis added].[10]

Newton does not mention having permission to take the seated statues from the Sacred Way at the Temple of Apollo Didymeus at Branchidae (see Chapter 8).[11] Indeed, he says little about permissions during his eight-year appointment by the Foreign Office, during which time he was instructed to obtain antiquities for the British Museum.

Permissions to take antiquities from ancient sites were requested and obtained from the Turkish government, for example at Halicarnassus (Chapter 8). Sometimes the scope of the permission granted was clearly exceeded, for example at Xanthus (Chapter 15). The existence of permissions for some excavations can be seriously doubted, for example at Carthage (Chapter 14). At some sites there clearly was no permission to remove all that was taken, for example at Priene (Chapter 9) and Cyrene (Chapter 13).

The excavations discussed in Part II of this book were instigated by the trustees of the British Museum and funded by the British government. There is no harm in this, provided the excavations were conducted with permission and within its terms. Therefore, whenever it is maintained that antiquities were collected by adventurous archaeologists, explorers and extraordinary individuals, it signals that there was no permission or, if any, the permission did not permit the removal of what was taken. In these instances, the trustees distanced themselves from the excavations by creating the fiction that the antiquities were taken by individuals acting on their own.

---

[9] Newton, *Travels and Discoveries in the Levant*, vol. II, p. 27.

[10] Newton, *Travels and Discoveries in the Levant*, vol. II, p. 27.

[11] Newton, *Travels and Discoveries in the Levant*, vol. II, p. 231.

There is another reason why the trustees distanced themselves from excavations *even* in cases where permission *was* obtained. It is because the mutilation and destruction of ancient sites under the specific directions of the trustees of the British Museum was barbaric and shameful.

CHAPTER 8

Halicarnassus, Cnidus and Branchidae: Charles Newton

Newton took antiquities for the British Museum from Halicarnassus, Cnidus and Branchidae. Halicarnassus is present-day Bodrum in Turkey. Cnidus (or Knidos) is south of Bodrum on the tip of the Datça peninsula. Branchidae (known as Didyma) is eleven miles south of the ancient port city of Miletus on the western coast of Turkey.

In April 1856, Newton was appointed Vice-Consul at Bodrum and held the post for three years.[1] Newton went to Bodrum for one reason only – to excavate and dismantle the remains of the Mausoleum of Halicarnassus, one of the Seven Wonders of the Ancient World.

From 1856, Newton sent regular progress reports to the Earl of Clarendon (Foreign Secretary and trustee of the British Museum). The reports reveal excavations at Halicarnassus on a massive scale.[2] In December 1857, Newton reported that since 'September 30, the excavations at the Mausoleum have been carried on without interruption, and with an average force of 100 Turkish labourers daily'.[3] He was assisted by 'a party of fifty sailors' from HMS *Gorgon*, who landed 'with picks and shovels'.[4] He was also assisted by Lieutenant R. M. Smith, a Royal Engineer, and a detachment of four Royal Engineer sappers.[5]

---

[1] *The Foreign Office List* (London: Harrison, 1869), p. 141.

[2] *Papers respecting the excavations at Budrum.* UK PP, 1857–58 [2359] [2378].

[3] Treasury Register of Papers. Public Offices A–M 1857. British Museum. Enclosure No. 12. TNA, T 2/238, p.27.

[4] Newton, *Travels and Discoveries in the Levant*, vol. II, p. 70.

[5] Letter from J. Burgoyne (War Office) to E. Hammond (Treasury), 7 June 1860. TNA, ADM 1/5745.

The Admiralty recorded:

> Excavations at Bodrum and Cnidus. F.O. [Foreign Office] requests that a vessel may be put at disposal ... and that a detachment of Sappers and Miners may be embarked therein.[6]

Newton wrote:

> The ship appointed for this service was *Gorgon* ... with a crew of 150 men ... Lieutenant R. M. Smith was the officer in command of Sappers.[7]

As evidenced by the following Admiralty entry (relating to victualling stores supplied to the expedition), when it came to taking antiquities there was hands-on involvement across government departments – the Foreign Office, the Treasury, the Admiralty and the Colonial Office:

> Foreign Office state that only 52 rations are chargeable to them and that the value of the rations are chargeable to the Colonial Office (511 rations) & Acct. Gen. Accountant General ... submits that the Colonial Office be again asked & the Paymaster General ... requested to receive the amount from the Colonial Office instead of the Foreign Office.[8]

Newton took Greco-Roman sculptures from Halicarnassus. These included a group of Bacchus and Ariadne; a draped female torso; a winged female figure; a Roman lady; fragment of a relief; a circular altar; and an iconic male head.[9] He also took Roman mosaics, thirty-three of which are described in an 1876 British Museum publication.[10] In 2019, eleven of the mosaics from Halicarnassus were on the walls of the British Museum West Stairs and another one was in Room 70.

---

[6] Admiralty Digest 1856, Case 90a British Museum. TNA, ADM 12/624.

[7] Newton, *Travels and Discoveries in the Levant*, vol. 2, p. 68.

[8] TNA, ADM 12/686.

[9] *Synopsis of the Contents of the British Museum: Department of Greek and Roman Antiquities: Greco-Roman Sculptures*, Part II (London: Printed by Order of the Trustees, 1876).

[10] 'Mosaics from Halicarnassus (Bodrum)', *Synopsis of the Contents of the British Museum*, Part II, pp. 67–75.

Newton wrote that he took ten seated statues from the Sacred Way at the Temple of Apollo Didymeus, the ancient site of Branchidae.[11] In 2018, four of the ten statues were on public display in the museum, and a reconstruction drawing showed 'how the statues *might* originally have been arranged. It represents a shrine on the Sacred Way excavated between 1984 and 1986' [emphasis added].[12]

It is disingenuous of the British Museum to rely on excavations in the 1980s. The museum knows *exactly* how the ten seated statues were arranged because Newton wrote 'I took photographs of them all'.[13] Furthermore, Corporal Spackman, a Royal Engineer with Newton, made a 'Plan of ground, Sacred Way, Branchidae' and 'Fourteen drawings of Statues from the Sacred Way, Branchidae'.[14] In addition, two of the photographs 'of the Seated Figures from the Sacred Way, Branchidae' are reproduced in a book written by Newton.[15] The two photographs are part of 'Upwards of 300 photographic negatives containing views of sculptures, excavations and scenery at Bodrum, Cnidus and Branchidae taken by Corporal Spackman R.E.'.[16]

Newton made a beeline for Branchidae because he was aware of its archaeological importance. Branchidae is one of the ancient sites that was documented by the Society of Dilettanti in 1764 (see Chapter 9).

In 1858, Newton made the spurious claim that he found the ten statues at Branchidae 'partially buried in the soil. In some cases only the base of the neck was visible; in others the soil did not rise higher than the lap of the figure'.[17] Newton lied because the statues were clearly visible in 1764 when the Society of Dilettanti's expedition to Branchidae documented 'the Sacred Way ... with the seated figures'.[18] Furthermore, in 1821,

---

[11] Newton, *Travels and Discoveries in the Levant*, vol. II, p. 231.

[12] British Museum, Room 13, captioned photographed 14 February 2019.

[13] Newton, *Travels and Discoveries in the Levant*, vol. II, p. 149.

[14] *Further Papers respecting the Excavations at Budrum and Cnidus: Presented to the House of Lords by Command of Her Majesty* (London: Harrison and Sons, 1859). UK PP, Series 2 [2575], pp. 102 & 103.

[15] C. T. Newton, *A History of Discoveries at Halicarnassus, Cnidus and Branchidae* (London: Day and Son, 1862), vol. I, plates LXXIV & LXXV.

[16] 'Mr. Newton's Discoveries in Asia Minor', *The Times*, 5 September 1859, p. 9.

[17] Newton, *Travels and Discoveries in the Levant*, vol. II, p. 149.

[18] *History of the Society of the Society of Dilettanti* compiled by Lionel Cust (London: Macmillan, 1898), p. 87.

thirty years before Newton went to Branchidae, the Society of Dilettanti published an engraving of five of the seated statues.[19] Newton was aware of the Dilettanti's publication because he wrote 'I am going tomorrow with one of the photographers to Branchidae ... where there are remains of a beautiful temple ... published by the Dilettanti Society. Near this temple *is an avenue of seated colossal figures*' [emphasis added].[20]

Newton claimed he uncovered the statues, and wrote to the Earl of Clarendon that they were now vulnerable:

> Though I placed two Turks on guard on the site while I was excavating, two of the statues which I had uncovered were disfigured in the night in the same barbarous manner ... such interesting monuments of early Greek art as these should on no account be left in their present situation, exposed to mutilation, and ultimate destruction, at the hands of the barbarous inhabitants of this district.[21]

This was nonsense. The statues had been left well alone for centuries before being documented by the Society of Dilettanti.

Clarendon, wearing his British Museum trustee hat, agreed to Newton's request and the statues were transported to the museum by HMS *Supply* in case numbers 311–321, 374 and 375.[22]

The seated statues had survived on the Sacred Way *since the sixth century BC.* In 1859, the ten statues were taken to the British Museum and put in storage. In 2019, the museum displayed four of the ten statues (Room 13) without reference to the other six in the collection and without stating they had been taken by Newton.

The ten statues will never be shown as a group, not only for want of space at the museum but also because there is clearly embarrassment at the museum. Why else would it exhibit four without reference to the other six and have the display label read:

---

[19] *Antiquities of Ionia published by The Society of Dilettanti* (London: W. Bulmer, 1821), p. 29.
[20] Letter from C. T. Newton to E. Hammond (Foreign Office), 19 October 1857, TNA, FO 78/1335, pp. 221–3.
[21] Letter from C. T. Newton to Earl of Clarendon, 22 March 1857, PP UK PP, 1859 [2575], p. 5.
[22] *Further Papers respecting the Excavations at Budrum and Cnidus: Presented to the House of Lords by Command of Her Majesty.* UK PP, Series 2 [2575]), pp. 38 and 99.

This reconstruction drawing shows how the statues might originally have been arranged. It represents a shrine on the Sacred Way excavated between 1984 and 1986.[23]

Museums are custodians, with a duty to show the objects in their collections honestly and transparently.

In 1861, Newton wrote a book with the title page:

A HISTORY OF DISCOVERIES AT

Halicarnassus, Cnidus & Branchidæ.

Being the Results of an Expedition sent to Asia Minor by H.M. Government in 1856.

BY

C.T. NEWTON, ESQ.

Director of the Expedition – Keeper of the Greek & Roman Antiquities, British Museum.

Assisted by R.P. Pullan, Esq. F.R.I.B.A.[24]

In the following year, Newton's book was reprinted but with two significant changes in the title. The following words were deleted: 'Being the Results of an Expedition sent to Asia Minor by H.M. Government in 1856 … Director of the Expedition'.

The changes were an attempt to conceal the roles of both the British government and Newton. However, the change in the title was futile because there is a superabundance of irrefutable evidence to support the original title. The government *did* fund the expedition and Newton *was* its director.

Newton could not take tons of antiquities from Halicarnassus, Cnidus and Branchidae without the full support and backing of the government.

The Foreign Office instructed the Admiralty to put HMS *Supply* at Newton's disposal and the ship ferried him between Malta, Bodrum, Cnidus, Smyrna and the Greek Islands. Between 26 November 1859 and 24 September 1860 Newton was on

---

[23] BM Room 13, display label photographed 14 February 2019.

[24] *A History of Discoveries at Halicarnassus, Cnidus and Branchidae Being the Results of an Expedition sent to Asia Minor by H.M. Government in 1856.* By C.T. Newton Director of the Expedition, M.A. Keeper of the Greek and Roman Antiquities, British Museum. Assisted by R.P. Pullan, Esq. F.R.I.B.A. (2 vols.) (London: Day and Son, 1861).

board HMS *Supply* for fifty-one days. The Admiralty sent the Foreign Office a schedule enquiring 'whether the expense of the entertainment [of Newton] is to be borne by the Public?'[25]

It is claimed that Newton received limited financial support from the British Museum, was kept 'painfully short of funds', received funds from Stratford Canning, and requested £2,000.[26]

In fact, Newton was exceedingly well-funded, as is testified by the 'note' to the estimate in public accounts laid before parliament:

BRITISH MUSEUM (PURCHASES)

An Estimate of the sum that will be required in the year 1858, ending 31 March 1859, for the purchase of objects for the Museum.

Five Thousand Pounds.

Note – this sum is for the purpose of defraying the *cost of excavations carried on by Vice-Consul Newton at Bodrum* (Halicarnassus) and for the conveyance to the Museum of the Marbles and interesting objects of ancient art discovered by that gentleman, as explained in the Papers laid before Parliament in the present Session [emphasis added].[27]

Two letters from the Treasury to the Foreign Office in 1858 explain how the government paid for 'carrying on antiquarian researches at Bodrum the ancient Halicarnassus, & in the Island of Cnidus'.

In the first letter, the Treasury confirmed that Lord Clarendon was refunded £3,133.19s.11d, advanced by him to the Bodrum Expedition. The Treasury charged this to 'Civil Contingencies'.[28]

In the second letter the Treasury reported:
- the 'Account of Naval Services' was credited with £644.14s.5d for supplies issued by the Naval Department to the expedition from 1857 to 1859;

---

[25] Letter from [indistinct name] to E. Hammond, 18 December 1858. TNA, FO 78/1490, pp. 139–40.

[26] Jenkins, *Keeping their Marbles*, p. 173.

[27] Public works and buildings. Estimates, etc., civil services. For the year ending 31 March 1859. UK PP, 1857–8 (162-I-VII), p. 29.

[28] Letter from C. E. Trevelyan to E. Hammond, 1 March 1858, Treasury Book of Out-Letters to Foreign Office. TNA, T 12/2.

- the 'Account of Army Services' was credited with £771.11s.8d for stores supplied by the War Department;
- the War Department received £592.6s.3d on account of the pay for 'the Detachment of Royal Engineers, under Lieutenant Smith';
- Newton was paid 'the sum of £103.3s.10d being the amount which appears to be due to him on account of expenses connected with the Bodrum Expedition'; and
- £1,284 was advanced from 'Civil Contingencies'.[29]

This letter from the Treasury underlies the extent to which the Army and Navy were involved in taking antiquities for the British Museum. Further, it establishes that not all government funding paid out to take antiquities for the British Museum went through the museum's accounts.

Newton's expedition lasted three years, during which time the Treasury asked the Admiralty for estimates of expenses and demanded reports from the trustees of the museum to assure parliament that the money was being well spent by Newton. The Treasury then authorised the continuance of Newton's operations.[30]

Newton wrote that he had been 'instructed' by the Foreign Office to take antiquities for the British Museum. Naturally, therefore, the government paid. Government funding was the only way Newton could employ 100 workmen a day, for months on end, take 385 cases of marble and transport the cases to England. Newton's funds were inexhaustible – until the government called a halt on 26 April 1859:

> Cnidus Expedition ordered home.
>   F.O. reports that Mr. Newton has been ordered to stop his operations and to prepare for instant embarkation with his party, stores, and antiquities.[31]

Having taken all the antiquities he could lay his hands on, Newton returned to the British Museum where he remained for twenty-seven years. In 1861, he was appointed Keeper of

---

[29] Letter from C. E. Trevelyan to E. Hammond, 6 March 1858, Treasury Book of Out-Letters to Foreign Office. TNA, T 12/2

[30] Books of Out-Letters. TNA, T 12/1, p. 236.

[31] Case 90a British Museum. TNA, ADM 12/672.

Greek and Roman Antiquities, a post he held until he retired in 1886. As Keeper, Newton personally orchestrated the taking of antiquities from Priene (Chapter 9), Cyrene (Chapter 13) and Cyprus (Chapter 18).

In 2012, a group of thirty lawyers from Bodrum announced that they were going to the European Court of Human Rights to reclaim sculptures originally from the Mausoleum of Halicarnassus that are held by the British Museum.[32]

---

[32] Dalya Alberge, 'Turkey turns to human rights law to reclaim British Museum sculptures', *The Guardian*, 8 December 2012 <www.theguardian.com/culture/2012/dec/08/turkey-british-museum-eculptures 16/03/2016>.

CHAPTER 9

Priene: Charles Newton and R. P. Pullan

In 1871, Charles Newton, at that time Keeper of Greek and Roman Antiquities, wrote in the British Museum Accounts that the Society of Dilettanti donated to the museum a considerable collection of antiquities from the Temple of Athena Polias in Priene on the west coast of Turkey.[1] However, Newton's claim was a fiction and part of an elaborate cover-up. He took the antiquities himself by a subterfuge that has gone undetected until revealed in this book. This chapter explains:

- what was taken from the Temple of Athena Polias;
- the roles of the trustees of the British Museum, the Treasury and the Admiralty in taking the antiquities;
- how the antiquities were transported from Priene to the British Museum's door; and
- why the Society of Dilettanti did not take them.

In 1869, eighty tons of marble, packed in 110 cases, were taken from the Temple of Athena Polias to the British Museum.

In 1870, eight engravings of objects taken from Priene were published. These included a 'colossal foot and head', 'heads of the Macedonian period', and a 'pilaster'.[2] However, what was taken is documented in three British Museum sources:

- Newton's two-page description in the 1871 British Museum Accounts of objects allegedly donated by the Dilettanti Society;[3]

---

[1] British Museum Accounts for year ended 31 March 1871. UK PP, 1871 (272), pp. 15–16.

[2] 'The Priene Exhibition', *The Graphic*, 12 November 1870, p. 468.

[3] British Museum Accounts for year ended 31 March 1871. UK PP, 1871 (272), pp. 15–16.

- forty-one monumental marble inscriptions from the Temple of Athena Polias listed in Newton's *The Collection of Ancient Greek Inscriptions in the British Museum;*[4] and
- *The Mausoleum and Sculptures of Halicarnassus and Priene in the British Museum.*[5]

The trustees of the British Museum, the Treasury and the Admiralty were all involved in taking the antiquities.

The trustees sent Newton to the Temple of Athena Polias twice to personally supervise what to take for the museum. This is recorded by E. L. Hicks, who was at Priene and wrote, 'I have been assured by Mr. C. T. Newton, who visited Priene in 1869 and 1870 ... the work then progressing under the guidance of Mr. Newton'.[6]

The Admiralty recorded three letters under 'British Museum – Antiquities at Smyrna excavated at Priene'.[7] The first letter establishes that the British Museum gave directions regarding transportation of the antiquities two years *before* the alleged donation to the museum by the Society of Dilettanti:

> Thanks of British Museum for the orders given to the Commander in Chief in the Mediterranean to convey them [from Smyrna] to Malta in a Ship of War (14 June 1869).

The second letter establishes the number of cases taken from Priene;

> Request that 110 cases lying at Smyrna may be conveyed to Malta ... (13 July 1869).

The third letter implicates the Treasury:

> Treasury offer to sanction or repay any expenditure which may be incurred ... (16 September 1869).

---

[4] Newton, ed., *The Collection of Ancient Greek Inscriptions in the British Museum*, Part III.

[5] A. H. Smith, *The Mausoleum and Sculptures of Halicarnassus and Priene in the British Museum* (London: Printed by Order of the Trustees, 1900).

[6] E. L. Hicks, 'Judith and Holofernes', *The Journal of Hellenic Studies*, vol. 6 (1885), pp. 261–94; p. 267.

[7] Admiralty Digest 1869, Case 90a British Museum. TNA, ADM 12/835.

The Treasury is further embroiled by George Hamilton (permanent secretary at the Treasury), who directed the Admiralty

> that immediate steps should be taken to bring home a number of cases containing very valuable antiquities which have been recently acquired from the ruins of Priene ... it should be done soonest and if an HM Ship was not available the Admiralty should charter a private vessel ... about 110 separate boxes ... the cases should be transported as belonging to H.M. Government.[8]

Therefore the Treasury was in no doubt that the cases belonged to the government and not to the Society of Dilettanti.

The Treasury recorded the following correspondence:

> Priene Ruins:
> – Steps taken to bring home certain antiquities lying at Smyrna. 69/14983*.
> – HMS 'Antelope' engaged. 15184*.[9]

On 14 October 1869, the Treasury notified the trustees of the British Museum 'that all of the antiquities from the ruins of Smyrna have been conveyed to Malta'.[10]

The British Consul at Smyrna confirmed the British Museum's involvement in two letters to the British Ambassador in Constantinople. In the first, commenting on a Turkish order to stop all excavations for antiquities, he wrote:

> the order will prove detrimental to the excavations already advanced, of Mr. Wood at Ephesus, Mr. Pullan at Sokia [sixteen miles from Priene] and Mr. Dennis at Sardis ... *heavy expenses have been incurred on their behalf by the British Museum* [emphasis added].[11]

---

[8] Letter from George Hamilton to the Secretary to the Admiralty, 2 September 1869, Treasury: Books of Out-Letters to the Admiralty 1865–1870. TNA, T 5/5, p. 509.

[9] * indicates year [1869] and letter number in destroyed Treasury correspondence file. Subject Registers. A–Z. 1866–1870, Science & Art. TNA, T 108/4, p. 22.

[10] Letter from William Law to the Trustees of the British Museum, 14 October 1869. Treasury: General Out-Letters Book 1869. TNA, T 27/161.

[11] Letter from Robert W. Cumberbatch to Henry Elliot, 3 March 1869. TNA, FO 78/2073.

In the second letter, the Consul wrote (in respect of 'the hundred cases of antiquities' left in his charge by Mr. Pullan) that 'from the communication I have received by telegram from the British Museum I expect that a Ship of War will shortly arrive to convey the above mentioned cases to England'.[12]

The following is how eighty tons of marble from the Temple of Athena Polias was transported from Priene to the British Museum.

First, the cases were taken from Priene to the nearest port, Smyrna (present-day Izmir, on Turkey's west coast). Newton was in charge of the operation.

> Aided by the experience of Mr. Newton of the British Museum these statues were conveyed ... to the nearest point on the Smyrna and Aidin railway. From Smyrna they were transmitted to England on board a ship of war.[13]

The Admiralty recorded the following request from the British Museum: 'Antiquities from Smyrna. British Museum requests may be brought to England in a Man of War.'[14]

At Smyrna, the 110 cases were loaded on HMS *Antelope* as recorded in the ship's log book.[15] *Antelope* arrived at Malta on 20 September 1869.[16]

At Malta the cases were loaded on HMS *Simoon*: 'Monday the 24 January 1870 at Malta ... Employed getting in Antiquities *for British Museum*' [emphasis added].[17] Therefore, even onboard ship in Malta it was *known* that the cases from Priene belonged to the British Museum and not to the Society of Dilettanti.

The expenses incurred by the Admiralty at Malta were charged *directly* to the trustees of the British Museum, not to the Society of Dilettanti. The Appropriation Account for the sums granted by parliament for Navy services includes:

> Trustees of the British Museum: For wages of Artificers at Malta in 1869–70 for Packing Antiquities in Her

---

[12] Letter from Robert W. Cumberbatch to Henry Elliot, 9 June 1869. TNA, FO 195/942, pp. 99–100.

[13] 'The Priene Exhibition', *The Graphic*, 12 November 1870, p. 466.

[14] Admiralty Digest 1867, Case 90a British Museum. TNA, ADM 12/801.

[15] HMS *Antelope* Log Book, 10, 14 and 15 September 1869. TNA, ADM 53/9633.

[16] Case 90a British Museum. TNA, ADM 12/835; *Antelope*'s Log Book. TNA, ADM 53/9633.

[17] *Simoon*. TNA, ADM 53/9570.

Majesty's Ship *Simoon* and Repairing Packing Cases and
Transport of the same ...[18]

HMS *Simoon* arrived at Portsmouth with 'about 80 tons of
Antiquities'.[19] The Admiralty notified the Treasury that
the antiquities from Smyrna were 'consigned to the British
Museum'.[20] Finally, the Admiralty recorded the thanks of the
trustees: 'Greek and Roman Antiquities safe arrival of reported.
Thanks of Trustees of British Museum (16 March)'.[21]

It was the trustees, not the Society of Dilettanti, who thanked
the Admiralty.

In 1900, A. H. Smith (senior curator at the British Museum),
in a fiction whose origin may have preceded him, asserted that
the marbles from Priene were transported to England by the
generosity of John Ruskin, an art critic.[22] However, the 110 cases
of marble from Priene were transported by the Admiralty and
the Treasury paid the bill.

The Society of Dilettanti was established in 1732 as a small
private society of gentlemen. It was a dining club for those who
had travelled to Italy and Greece. Its members appreciated
antiquities in situ. The society did not take eighty tons of marble
from Priene. The society never removed tons of antiquities
from ancient sites. This is clearly established in the minutes and
records in the authoritative *History of the Society of Dilettanti*.[23]

In 1764, the society sent an expedition to Priene during
which no antiquities were taken. The society published *Ionian
Antiquities* in 1769, followed by a second volume in 1797 and
a revised edition (*Antiquities of Ionia*) in 1821.[24] The three
oversize volumes include large scale engravings and meticulous
architectural drawings. The 1821 edition has eighteen plates of
the Temple of Athena Polias at Priene.[25]

---

[18] Navy: Appropriation Account 1870–71. UK PP (72), p. 90.

[19] Case 90a British Museum. TNA, ADM 12/856.

[20] Admiralty. TNA, T 2/286.

[21] Case 90a British Museum. TNA, ADM 12/856.

[22] Smith, *The Mausoleum and Sculptures of Halicarnassus and Priene in the British
Museum*, p. 144.

[23] Cust, *History of the Society of Dilettanti.*

[24] *Ionian Antiquities, published by order of The Society of Dilettanti* (London: printed by
T. Spilsbury and W. Haskell, 1769).

[25] *Antiquities of Ionia published by The Society of Dilettanti* (London: printed by W.
Bulmer et al, 1821), Chapter II.

All the drawings from the 1764 expedition 'were deposited by the Society of Dilettanti with the Trustees of the British Museum'.[26] The Society can never have imagined how the trustees would use their drawings. Priene was one of the ancient sites targeted for 'prestigious antiquities' by the trustees.

Newton became a member of the Society of Dilettanti in 1863.[27] The contention in this book is that he arranged for the architect Richard Popplewell Pullan to be sent to Priene by the Society to make drawings. Newton used this as an opportunity to conduct a covert operation to take antiquities for the British Museum. Ten years before going to Priene, Pullan assisted Newton in Bodrum where he made architectural drawings of the mausoleum before Newton had it dismantled. Pullan is named in the title of Newton's book *A History of Discoveries at Halicarnassus, Cnidus and Branchidae by C. T. Newton ... Assisted by R. P. Pullan, Esq. F.R.I.B.A.*

In 1868, the Society of Dilettanti commissioned Pullan to make a survey at Priene.[28] He was to make drawings; he was not instructed to take eighty tons of marble or any antiquities. Newton went to Priene twice while Pullan was allegedly making drawings when in fact the two of them were taking 110 cases of marble.

The Society of Dilettanti had neither the wish nor the financial resources to remove and transport eighty tons of marble. In 1868, the society's only expenditure on 'Contributions to Art' were 'Printing Report on Priene £5 11s.' and 'Mr. Pullan for Priene investigations £313 10s.'. In 1869–70, the society spent £400 on 'Priene and Smintheus', then nothing from 1871 through to 1876.[29] In 1871, the society was obliged to defer a proposed publication for want of funds.

The Society of Dilettanti was oblivious of the fact that eighty tons of marble had been taken by Newton and Pullan from the Temple of Athena Polias.

---

[26] Cust, *History of the Society of Dilettanti*, p. 106.

[27] 'List of Members of the Society of Dilettanti', in Cust's *History of the Society of Dilettanti*, p. 301.

[28] Cust, *History of the Society of Dilettanti*, p. 201.

[29] Cust, *History of the Society of Dilettanti*, reissued with supplementary chapter, etc. (London: Macmillan, 1914), p. 353.

* * *

In 2013 the Museum of Archaeology (Istanbul) displayed a map of the west coast of Turkey, showing a chronological 'History of Research' from 1720 to 1984 along with the names of excavators and precisely what they took.[30] The following are two *sequential* entries:

> 1842/1843 – C. Texier; first excavations at Magnesia [now Ortaklar, nine miles south-east of Ephesus]. He takes 41 figured frieze blocks, which are 40 metres long and some of the architectural elements to Paris.

> 1891/1893 – C. Humann; starts excavations again. Temenos of Artemision ... at the end of these excavations the friezes are taken to Berlin (Pergamon Museum) and Istanbul Archaeological Museums.

Between the above entries there should be a record of the excavations at Priene in 1869–70 with details of the contents of 110 cases taken from the Temple of Athena Polias to the British Museum.

The fact that the Museum of Archaeology has no record suggests that Turkish permission was never granted for excavations at Priene, and that Newton's covert operation went under the radar, as intended.

* * *

On 3 March 1869, the British Consul at Smyrna wrote to the British Ambassador in Constantinople and informed him that Pullan was excavating at Sokia (Söke).[31] This is sixteen miles from Priene. But the previous day the ambassador wrote to the Turkish government that Pullan was excavating at 'Calabiche'.[32] It is unclear whether the Turkish authorities appreciated where Pullan was excavating, but they clearly had no idea what he took.

On 9 June 1869, the Consul at Smyrna wrote to the ambassador and informed him that the local customs officer was demanding to inspect the contents of Pullan's cases. He

---

[30] The Museum of Archaeology, visited by the author 2013.

[31] Letter from R. W. Cumberbatch to H. Elliot, 3 March 1869. TNA, FO 78/2073.

[32] Letter from H. Elliot to Ismail Pasha, 2 March 1869. TNA, FO 78/2073.

suggested the ambassador should 'demand' that orders be given 'immediately' by the authorities in Constantinople 'to the Customs of Smyrna to permit the hundred cases of antiquities to pass without any impediment as it would be impossible to have the cases examined'.[33] There is no evidence that the cases from Priene were inspected.

* * *

In the authoritative *History of the Society of Dilettanti* there is no record of the Society having *ever* sought permission to take antiquities from *anywhere.*

If the British Museum or government had obtained a permission to excavate at Priene, then Newton would not have needed to create the fiction of the donation from the Society of Dilettanti. If permission had been granted *to anyone,* then the excavations at Priene in 1869–70 would be a matter of record and known to the Museum of Archaeology, Istanbul.

* * *

Newton clearly lied and spread misinformation about what he did at Priene. In 1885, E. L. Hicks, who knew Newton but was unaware that he took eighty tons of marble, thereby mutilating the temple, wrote of the Temple of Athena Polias:

> I have been assured by Mr. C. T. Newton, who visited Priene in 1869 and 1870 ... that when the site had been cleared by Mr. Pullan, the ruin was still *very beautiful* [emphasis added].[34]

Hicks added:

> It is sad to think that *the intelligent interest* shown in a ruin by Western archaeologists has usually the effect of hastening its *utter destruction.* No sooner had the English explorers [Newton and Pullan] bidden farewell to Priene, than the stonemasons of the nearest Greek village established themselves among the ruins ... the ruins became a convenient quarry [emphasis added].[35]

---

[33] Letter from Robert W. Cumberbatch to H. Elliot, 9 June 1869. TNA, FO 195/942, pp. 99–100.

[34] Hicks, 'Judith and Holofernes', p. 267.

[35] Hicks, 'Judith and Holofernes', p. 267.

Little did Hicks know that the *utter destruction* was down to Newton and Pullan.

It was a common tactic to blame locals for the destruction of ancient sites after they were devastated under directions of the trustees of the British Museum. The threat posed by local barbarians was used as a justification for 'saving' antiquities. Nathan Davis did this at Carthage (see Chapter 14). Newton did this with regard to the statues on the Sacred Way at the Temple of Apollo Didymeus at Branchidae (see Chapter 8). He spread the same falsehood at Priene to cover the barbaric act of destruction committed there.

What happened to the eighty tons of marble in 110 cases taken from the Temple of Athena Polias?

The answer is that it went directly to the British Museum stores where, with few exceptions, it has been since it was taken in 1869.

In 2019, only six objects with the provenance of the Temple of Athena Polias were on public display in the British Museum, each with the erroneous caption 'Presented by the Society of Dilettanti'.

In 2019, the British Museum online collection database listed 576 objects from Priene with the provenance 'Society of Dilettanti Charitable Trust?', and the trust's biographical details given as 'institution/organization, 1732 ... also known as Society of Dilettanti: Society of Dilettanti Charitable Trust'.[36] However, The Society of Dilettanti Charitable Trust is a charity established in England on 28 November 1977 (Charity No. 274838). This is over one hundred years after the alleged donation by the Society of Dilettanti.

The fiction of the donation from the Society of Dilettanti was part of a clever scheme at Priene. Newton, and others at the British Museum and in government departments, imagined the scheme would be undetectable. However, none can have anticipated that one day the following would be placed in The National Archives: Admiralty primary sources (recording the subject matter of every correspondence with the trustees of the British Museum; see Chapter 26); HM Ships' log books; and Foreign Office and Treasury records.

The sources at The National Archives are incriminating and, in the case of Priene, shine a light on one of the numerous

---

[36] British Museum Online. Last accessed 8 January 2019.

acts of vandalism personally directed by Newton, a keeper at the British Museum. Newton's other acts of vandalism are described in his books as 'his discoveries'.

Newton was financed throughout by the British government. Everything he did was sanctioned and approved by the trustees of the museum. The vast quantities plundered are hoarded in storage at the British Museum where there will *never* be enough space to display the antiquities (see Chapter 22).

* * *

Imagine for a moment a group of foreigners going to Stonehenge in 1869 (Queen Victoria had been on the throne for thirty-two years) and, without permission, excavated it, cut the stones into manageable sizes, packed them in cases and put them in storage in another country in perpetuity.

This was the fate of the Temple of Athena Polias. It was mutilated. Eighty tons of marble was packed into *110 cases*, which went directly to the British Museum stores.

The crime committed at Priene, covered up for one hundred and fifty years, has finally been exposed. What took place in 1869 was a barbaric and outrageous act of vandalism. The trustees of the British Museum knew this well. This is why the fiction of the donation from Society of Dilettanti was created and continues to this day.

It is important that what took place at Priene is remembered, but today, misinformation conceals the truth or it is ignored:

- *The British Museum: A History* (Wilson) has a single reference to the Temple of Athena Polias at Priene. It claims that the marbles were donated by the Society of Dilettanti;[37]
- *Archaeologists & Aesthetes in the Sculpture Galleries of the British Museum 1800–1939* (Ian Jenkins) names Pullan as one of the 'extraordinary individuals' but, with regard to Priene, there is a single sentence and it concerns the museum's lack of space for what he took from Priene;[38]
- *Keeping their Marbles* (Tiffany Jenkins) does not mention either the eighty tons of marbles taken from the Temple of Athena Polias or Priene; and

---

[37] Wilson, *The British Museum*, p. 150.
[38] Ian Jenkins, *Archaeologists & Aesthetes*, pp. 13–14.

- In Ian Jenkins' book, *Greek Architecture and its Sculpture in the British Museum,* it is claimed that Pullan made drawings at Priene, but 'sadly', after his departure, the Temple of Athena Polias was plundered for its stone; 'fortunately' Pullan brought back to the British Museum a number of sculptures, architectural fragments and inscriptions.[39]

Unimpeachable Treasury and Admiralty sources at The National Archives establish that *110 cases* of marble were taken from the Temple of Athena Polias to the British Museum.[40]

---

[39] Ian Jenkins, *Greek Architecture and Its Sculpture in the British Museum* (London: The British Museum Press 2006), p. 238.

[40] Books of Out-Letters to the Admiralty 1865–70. TNA, T 5/5, p. 509; Case 90a British Museum, ADM 12/835.

CHAPTER 10

Assyria and Babylon:
Austen Henry Layard and Henry Rawlinson

In 1834, the British Museum had a small collection of Assyrian and Babylonian antiquities which occupied 218 square feet. But in 1852, a new space of 4,710 square feet for the collection was described as being 'neither sufficient nor convenient'.[1] This chapter explains how the Assyrian and Babylonian collection grew exponentially and why, despite an increase of more than two thousand per cent, the space was still insufficient for the collection.

Austen Henry Layard and Henry Rawlinson are the archaeologists responsible for the growth of the collection. However, it has never been explained how Layard and Rawlinson acted under specific directions of the trustees of the British Museum in Assyria and were both funded by the British government.

The two were not the only excavators employed by the trustees in Assyria. According to Layard, Mr Ross, a British merchant in Mosul, was also requested by the trustees to carry on excavations in Assyria.[2]

Two sentences establish that Layard and Rawlinson were appointed by the trustees. The first sentence is Layard's: 'I accepted the request made to me by the Trustees of the British

---

[1] Enlargement of the British Museum, Report from Mr. Hoskins. UK PP, 1852 (557), p.15.

[2] Austen Henry Layard, *Nineveh and Its Remains*, 2 vols (London: John Murray, 1849), vol. 2, p. 139. The trustees subsequently employed Hormuzd Rassam in Assyria (see Chapter 19).

Museum ... to undertake the superintendence of a second expedition into Assyria'.[3] The second sentence is Rawlinson's brother's: 'The Trustees of the British Museum entrusted him [Henry Rawlinson] with a Commission to take charge of the excavations in Assyria, Babylonia, and Susiana, began some years before under their auspices ...'.[4]

Rawlinson was succinct in a letter to Panizzi, Principal Librarian at the museum, regarding 'the marbles which I have had the honour to obtain for the British Museum during my superintendence of the Assyrian excavations'.[5]

The extent of the British Museum's involvement in Assyrian excavations is highlighted by the following. Layard went on two expeditions to Assyria and wrote books on both. The title of the tenth chapter in his first book is 'Excavations on a *large scale* undertaken by the British Museum [emphasis added]'.[6] The title of the first chapter of his second book is 'The Trustees of the British Museum resume excavations at Nineveh'.[7]

Rawlinson's brother's book is peppered with references to the British Museum. For example, 'diggings on the Museum's account ... sculptures exhumed at the Museum's expense ... the Museum workmen were in possession of the palace [Kuyunjik] itself ...'.[8]

The British Museum appointed Layard and, after him, Rawlinson as superintendents in Assyria, but the trustees kept hands-on management.

Take as an example the appointment of artists. Layard described the trustees sending three successive artists to Assyria.[9] Their drawings were critically important because the trustees used them to pinpoint the antiquities to be taken during the course of excavations which lasted over a decade

---

[3] Austen H. Layard, M.P. *Discoveries in the ruins of Nineveh and Babylon: with travels in Armenia, Kurdistan and the desert: being the result of a second expedition undertaken for the Trustees of the British Museum*, 2 vols (London: John Murray, 1853), vol. 1, p. 2.

[4] George Rawlinson, M.A, F.R.G.S., *A Memoire of Major-General Sir Henry Creswicke Rawlinson* (London: Longmans, Green, and Co., 1898), p. 172.

[5] Letter from Sir Henry Rawlinson to the Principal Librarian British Museum, 2 April 1856. UK PP, 1857–58 (379), p. 14.

[6] Layard, *Nineveh and Its Remains*, vol. 1, p. 326.

[7] Layard, *Discoveries in the ruins of Nineveh and Babylon* (1953).

[8] Rawlinson, *A Memoire of Major-General Sir Henry Creswicke Rawlinson*, pp. 185–7.

[9] Mr. F. Cooper, Mr. Bell and Mr. Holder (Layard, *Discoveries in the ruins of Nineveh and Babylon*, pp. 2, 582, 584).

(see funding below). The drawings explain how Rawlinson was able to write to the museum, 'The marbles of the first shipment were principally obtained by me, according to *the wishes of the Trustees*' [emphasis added].[10]

The trustees' wishes were formulated by examining drawings. The trustees also supplied two of the three artists they sent to Assyria with photographic apparatus (see Chapter 23).

* * *

This is how British Museum excavations in Assyria were funded.

The first history of the British Museum (1870) candidly states that the Assyrian antiquities, partly discovered by Austen Henry Layard, were 'Excavated at the public charge, and under the joint direction of the Trustees of the British Museum and of the Secretary of State for Foreign Affairs'.[11]

The British Museum Accounts for 1847–8 include 'Received on account of Grant for excavations etc., in Kurdistan and transport of marbles'.[12] Kurdistan is in present-day Iraq, formerly Assyria. The title of Layard's first book includes 'travels in ... Kurdistan ... Being the result of a Second Expedition undertaken for THE TRUSTEES OF THE BRITISH MUSEUM'. The capital letters are Layard's (see below).

The British Museum received specific grants from the government for excavations in Assyria in 1847 and in *every* year until 1857. Thereafter, the museum received grants in 1864, 1867, 1869 and in every year from 1874 through to 1883 (with the exception of 1877 and 1882).

The grants are in British Museum Accounts (see Appendix 1). In 1852, the museum received £3,500 for 'Expenditure for excavations, etc., in Assyria, and transport of marbles'.[13] This was a significant amount because the museum's total annual grant in 1852 was £52,530.

The Treasury Register of Papers (T2 series at The National Archives) records the subject matter of all correspondence with the British Museum. It includes numerous requests from

---

[10] Letter from Sir Henry Rawlinson to the Principal Librarian British Museum, 2 April 1856. UK PP, 1857–58 (379), p. 14.

[11] Edwards, *Lives of The Founders of the British Museum*, p. 37.

[12] UK PP, 1847–48 (139), p. 4.

[13] UK PP, 1852 (238-I-VII), p. 5.

the museum for funding in Assyria.[14] British Museum requests specifically refer to Layard and Rawlinson. The following are two examples of requests recorded by the Treasury:

- In 1850, £2,000 for researches 'related to Mr. Layard's excavations at Nimrud';[15]
- In 1851, £500 on account to enable Colonel Rawlinson to undertake antiquarian researches in Asia Minor.[16]

In 1852, the Treasury recorded that the museum received a credit of '£500 – Col. Rawlinson researches in Assyria & Babylon' and a grant of £1,466 for Layard's activities on behalf of the museum in Assyria.[17]

Layard and Rawlinson (under directions of the British Museum) took the following from Assyria:

- twelve cases of Assyrian sculptures from Nimrud in 1847;[18]
- fifty-five cases in 1848;[19]
- 'nearly a hundred cases' from Nineveh, which Layard wrote he took in 1853;[20]
- 245 cases Rawlinson wrote were taken as follows: '128 cases received last year … 78 cases landed from the *Christiana Carnel* and 49 expected in the *Manuel*'.[21] Treasury recorded the arrival of *Christiana Carnel* from Basra with 'Assyrian Antiquities for the British Museum';[22]
- 'about 80 cases containing bricks, pottery, tables, cylinders, casts of inscriptions, and minor objects of art' from Rawlinson.[23] Treasury recorded a rival of

---

[14] TNA, T2/202; T2/206; T2/218; T2/226.

[15] Treasury Register of Papers 1850. British Museum. TNA, T 2/210.

[16] Treasury Register of Papers 1851. British Museum. TNA, T 2/214.

[17] Treasury Register of Papers 1852. British Museum. TNA, T 2/218.

[18] Treasury Register of Papers. British Museum. TNA, T 2/198.

[19] Treasury Register of Papers. British Museum. TNA, T 2/202.

[20] Layard, *Discoveries in the ruins of Nineveh and Babylon*, Part II, p. 463.

[21] Letter from Sir Henry Rawlinson to the Principal Librarian British Museum. UK PP, 1857–58 (379), p. 14.

[22] Books of Out-Letters to Board of Customs and Excise, 27 March 1856. TNA, T 11/110.

[23] Letter from Sir Henry Rawlinson to the Principal Librarian British Museum. UK PP, 1857–58 (379), p. 14.

Christiana Carnel from Basra with 'Assyrian Antiquities for the British Museum';[24] and

- an unknown number of cases containing 57,747 objects in the museum collection with the provenance from Hormuzd Rassam, who acted under directions of the trustees in Assyria (see Chapter 19).

When the Great Bull from Nineveh, weighing fifteen tons, arrived at the British Museum, it was claimed that the museum had received 'upwards of a hundred tons of sculpture'.[25] The bull arrived in 1850; therefore, the estimate did not include the approximate 100 cases from Nineveh taken by Layard in 1853 or the 325 cases taken by Rawlinson.

It is little wonder that in 1852 the additional space for the Assyrian and Babylonian collection was described as being 'neither sufficient nor convenient'.[26]

* * *

In a report to parliament outlining the museum's need for additional space, it was stated that 'the Assyrian researches have poured into the Museum'.[27] This was not an understatement. In the four years prior to 1852, when it was reported that the new space was 'neither sufficient nor convenient', *The Illustrated London News* had already published nine features with engravings titled 'Nimroud Sculptures' (see Appendix 3).

The Assyrian and Babylonian antiquities in the sources listed below are a shocking testament to the damage to cultural heritage inflicted on Nimroud, Nineveh, Khorsabad and Kuyunjik under *specific* directions of the trustees of the British Museum:

- the engravings of Assyrian objects in *twenty-nine* features in *The Illustrated London News* (see Appendix 3);

---

[24] Books of Out-Letters to Board of Customs and Excise, 27 March 1856. TNA, T 11/110.

[25] 'Shipping of the Great Bull from Nineveh', *The Illustrated London News*, 27 July 1850, p. 71.

[26] Enlargement of the British Museum, Report from Mr. Hoskins. UK PP, 1852 (557), p. 15.

[27] Enlargement of the British Museum, Report from Mr. Hoskins. UK PP, 1852 (557), p. 13.

- Layard's list of eighty-five sculptures taken to England;[28]
- Layard's list of forty-two ivories taken from Nimroud;[29] and
- the 600 woodcuts in Layard's books, many of the objects described as being 'now in the British Museum'.[30]

It is staggering what the trustees of the British Museum took from Assyria. In 1879, it was claimed that two thirds of the library of Nineveh was in the British Museum.[31]

* * *

The following is how antiquities from Nineveh (the ancient city in the centre of Mosul) were transported to the British Museum.

First they were taken by river raft to Basra. In 1849, the British Museum sent a request to the Admiralty:

> Nineveh Antiquities – Request from British Museum for the [HMS] *Meeanee* to be allowed to bring certain antiquities which have been excavated in the neighbourhood of Mosul from Bussorah [Basra] to England.[32]

Following the museum's request, the Admiralty gave 'Orders to the Captain of *Meeanee* to deliver the marbles to Mr. M. Doubleday of the British Museum'.[33]

In 1852, *Apprentice*, a merchant ship, transported Assyrian antiquities from Basra to London.[34] These merchant ships, chartered by the Admiralty, transported Assyrian antiquities to the British Museum: *Christiana Carnel, Firefly, Manuel* and *W. S. Lindsay*.

The Assyrian bas-reliefs in the museum (Rooms 9 and 10) and those exhibited at the museum's exhibition *I am Ashurbanipal King of the World, King of Assyria* (8 November 2018–24 February

---

[28] Layard, *Nineveh and Its Remains*, vol. 1, p. 395.
[29] Layard, *Nineveh and Its Remains*, vol. 1, p. 391–4.
[30] Layard, *Discoveries in the ruins of Nineveh and Babylon*, 2 vols (London: John Murray, 1853).
[31] 'The Libraries of the Assyrians and Babylonians', *The Times*, 3 June 1879, p. 11.
[32] Admiralty Digest 1849, Case 90a British Museum. TNA, ADM 12/512.
[33] Admiralty Digest 1849, Case 90a British Museum. TNA, ADM 12/512.
[34] 'The Nineveh Antiquities', *The Times*, 13 February 1852, p. 5; Case 90a British Museum. TNA, ADM 12/512.

2019) were visibly sawed to a standard size for ease of packing and transporting to England.

* * *

The British Museum: A History refers to 'Henry Layard' twice; thereafter, he is 'Layard'.[35] Layard wrote books and letters to *The Times*, calling himself either Austen H. Layard or A. H. Layard. Why would the most authoritative history of the British Museum by a former director not give Layard's first name 'Austen'?

This is pure speculation, but the reason may be so as not to draw attention to the title of Austen Henry Layard's book, in two parts, which states, in bold capitals, that his expedition was 'undertaken for THE TRUSTEES OF THE BRITISH MUSEUM':

DISCOVERIES

IN THE RUINS OF

NINEVEH AND BABYLON;

WITH TRAVELS IN ARMENIA, KURDISTAN AND THE

DESERT:

BEING THE RESULT OF A SECOND EXPEDITION
UNDERTAKEN FOR

THE TRUSTEES OF THE BRITISH MUSEUM

BY AUSTEN H. LAYARD, M.P.[36]

His book is not cited in the bibliography of *The British Museum: A History*, but two other books by 'A. H. Layard' are. *The British Museum: A History* explains that in 1851 'Henry Layard' published an abridged account of his first expedition in Murray's *Reading for Rail* series.[37] In fact, the abridgement is by Austen Henry Layard. Its title, *A popular account of discoveries at Nineveh*, does not mention the trustees of the museum.[38]

---

[35] Wilson, *The British Museum*, pp. 107–108.

[36] Austen Henry Layard, *Discoveries in the Ruins of Nineveh and Babylon … in Two Parts* (London: John Murray, 1853).

[37] Wilson, *The British Museum*, p. 108.

[38] Austen Henry Layard, *A Popular Account of Discoveries at Nineveh* (London, 1851).

* * *

At the British Museum exhibition *I am Ashurbanipal King of the World, King of Assyria,* which ran from November 2018 to February 2019, there was a display panel headed 'Layard and the British Museum'. The opening sentence read 'Layard's discoveries at Nimrud attracted funding from the British Museum'. This is correct. But what the panel does not convey is the fact that his excavations were 'undertaken for the Trustees of the British Museum' and funded throughout by the government.

The second sentence of the panel read, 'The Ottoman government authorised the British Ambassador [in Constantinople] to export *some of the sculptures* to England' [emphasis added]. Layard claimed the permission to do so was granted to him personally. He admitted that his name is not mentioned in the permission; he was referred to instead as an 'English gentleman'.[39]

There is not a court in any land that would construe the flimsy permission, dated 5 May 1846 and addressed to an 'English gentleman', as authority for the trustees of the British Museum to take the estimated over one hundred tons prior to 1850, and the unknown quantity over the next thirty years (evidenced by expenditure in British Museum Accounts).

The third, fourth and fifth sentences in the display panel described, in some detail, how the antiquities were transported to England – without mentioning HM Ships.

In a display case at the exhibition was a copy of Layard's book, but not the one whose title included in bold letters: 'Being the result of a Second Expedition undertaken for THE TRUSTEES OF THE BRITISH MUSEUM'. The book on display was Murray's *Reading for Rail* series abridged version, *A popular account of discoveries at Nineveh.*

* * *

In 1846, the Secretary of the British Museum sent a submission to the Treasury for a grant to excavate in Assyria, which made the following points:

---

[39] Gordon Waterfield, *Layard of Nineveh* (London: London: John Murray, 1963), pp. 141–2.

- 'Sir Stratford Canning (Britain's ambassador in Constantinople) commenced ... [in] 1845 ... excavations in the neighbourhood of Mosul and ... at Nimroud';
- 'His agent, Mr. Layard ... discovered ... the remains of a palace';
- 'It is difficult to overstate the archaeological importance of these discoveries';
- 'Canning ... [was] offering to the trustees the antiquities already found ... It will ... be necessary ... to discharge [Canning's] expenses ... which may amount to about £500';
- '[Canning's] offer will involve a total expenditure not exceeding £2,000. This sum ... will provide for expenses ... for excavations ... for packing the antiquities selected for the Museum ... and a moderate salary to Mr. Layard'.[40]

In response, the museum received a 'Special Parliamentary Grant' of £2,800 'for excavations etc., in Kurdistan [Assyria], and transport of marbles'.[41] Therefore, the grant covered £500 reimbursement to Canning, £2,000 for further excavations, and a £300 salary for Layard.

The fact that the government funded Layard's excavations is sometimes overlooked. For example, in 1998 an expert at the museum, relying on a Layard biographer, wrote that 'by June [1846] the funds ... advanced from Canning's own purse had run out and Layard was reduced to drawing money from his mother'.[42] Layard may well have asked his mother for money – children do that – but she did *not* pay for excavations in Assyria, and neither did Layard. The British government did. The evidence in British Museum Accounts is irrefutable (see Appendix 1).

* * *

---

[40] Letter from J. Forshall to the Treasury, 22 July 1846, *Report of Select Committee on Miscellaneous Expenditure*. UK PP, 1847–48 (543), p. 214.

[41] British Museum Accounts. UK PP, 1847–48 (139), p. 4.

[42] Richard D. Barnett, et al., *Sculptures from the Southwest Palace of Sennacherib at Nineveh* (London: British Museum Press, 1998), p. 3.

In 2019, the opening sentence of a display label in the British Museum read 'Much of the British Museum's Mesopotamian collections, including the material from Nimrud, was *brought* to England by Austen Henry Layard' [emphasis added].[43]

Museum display labels change. In 1963, a Layard biographer wrote that in the British Museum 'the Nimrud and Nineveh monuments are shown as *presented* by Layard' [emphasis added].[44] But Layard neither 'brought' nor 'presented' anything from Nimrud. It is a myth that Layard donated anything to the British Museum. The proof is as follows.

In 1846, the museum requested and received a grant from the Treasury to reimburse Canning for the Assyrian antiquities, which were obtained for Canning by Layard. The museum explained to the Treasury that Layard was Canning's agent.[45] Canning was fully reimbursed and the antiquities were taken over by the museum. At the same time, the museum received funds for '*a moderate salary to Mr. Layard*'.[46] Therefore, in 1845 Layard was an agent and in 1846 an employee. This establishes that none of the Assyrian antiquities were Layard's to give and that his alleged donations to the British Museum are a myth. The myth was created to distance the trustees from taking the antiquities.

In July 2019, Babylon was added to UNESCO's World Heritage list.

The role of the British Museum trustees and the government in taking tons upon tons of antiquities and, in doing so, devastating and destroying numerous Assyrian and Babylonian ancient sites has been whitewashed.

---

[43] 'Austen Henry Layard and the excavation of Nimrud', BM Room 7, photographed 14 February 2019.

[44] Waterfield, *Layard of Nineveh*, p. 142.

[45] Letter from J. Forshall to the Treasury, 22 July 1846, *Report of Select Committee on Miscellaneous Expenditure*. UK PP, 1847–48 (543), p. 214.

[46] Letter from J. Forshall to the Treasury, 22 July 1846, *Report of Select Committee on Miscellaneous Expenditure*. UK PP, 1847–48 (543), p. 214.

CHAPTER 11

Ephesus: John Turtle Wood

The Temple of Diana at Ephesus (also known as the Temple of Artemis) was one of the Seven Wonders of the Ancient World. Constructed in 500 BC, it was one of the few Greek temples built wholly of marble. It was destroyed in 356 BC, rebuilt, then rebuilt again. 'Its last rebuilding was at the expense of Alexander the Great (b. 366 BC–d. 323 BC) by his architect Dinocrates.'[1]

John Turtle Wood, acting under specific directions of the trustees of the British Museum, removed more than *sixty tons* of marble from the Temple of Diana over the course of *eleven years*, from May 1863 until 1874.

This chapter explains what was taken from the Temple of Diana, exposes the roles of the British government and trustees of the British Museum, gives a breakdown of Treasury funding over eleven years, details how the Admiralty transported over sixty tons from Ephesus, questions the existence of valid permissions to take what was taken, and highlights that the overall majority of what was taken went to, and remains in, storage.

* * *

In 1888, there was a dedicated 'Ephesus Room' in the British Museum. On public display were 'The sculptures and architectural members ... found by Mr. J. T. Wood, in the course of excavations on the site of the temple of Artemis [also known as the Temple of Diana] at Ephesus'.[2]

---

[1] George Aitchison, 'The Temple of Diana at Ephesus', *The Times*, 24 April 1890, p. 12.

[2] *Synopsis of the Contents of the British Museum: Department of Greek and Roman Antiquities: Greco-Roman Sculptures* (London: Printed by Order of the Trustees, 1876), Part II, pp. 9, 27, 36, 42.

The Ephesus Room included a sculptured drum from one of the columns of the temple with 'Thanatos and Hermes conducting Alkestis from Hades'; two pieces of similarly sculptured drums; remains of Herakles seated on a rock; a female figure; corner stone with a male overpowering a centaur; figures of a sheep and cow being led to sacrifice by Victories; the drum of an Ionic column; a torso of Silenus; Jupiter seated on a throne; Mercury; and a torso of Neptune. (In 2019, only the sculptured drum was on public display.)

A comprehensive study of the marbles taken from Ephesus was published in 1889 in *A Study of the Marbles from Ephesus in the British Museum. With suggestions on the restoration of the temple of Diana, as shewn in Mr. J. T. Wood's 'Discoveries at Ephesus'*.[3]

In addition to sculptures, the museum received 'four hundred and sixty-two [inscriptions] from Mr. Wood's excavations at Ephesus'.[4]

The British Museum also received more than 2,000 coins found by Wood at Ephesus. Mr. H. A. Grueber (Keeper of Coins and Medals, 1866–1912) wrote 'a full description of the coins in a pamphlet communicated to the Numismatic Society of London'.[5]

* * *

Wood wrote an account of his excavations at Ephesus in which he explained that they were 'carried on under the direction of the trustees of the British Museum'.[6]

To obtain the extraordinary quantities he took, Wood employed the following: in 1870–71, 'about one hundred workmen';[7] in 1872, 'about one hundred and fifty';[8] in March 1873, 'about 200 men';[9] and in 1873–4, 'more than three

---

[3] J. E. Goodchild, *A Study of the Marbles from Ephesus in the British Museum. With suggestions on the restoration of the temple of Diana, as shewn in Mr. J.T. Wood's 'Discoveries at Ephesus'* (Walthamstow: printed for private circulation, 1889).

[4] Newton ed., *The Collection of Ancient Greek Inscriptions in the British Museum*, Part I, Preface, n.p.

[5] J. T. Wood, F.S.A., *Discoveries at Ephesus, including the site and remains of the Great Temple of Diana* (London: Longmans, Green, and Co., 1877), pp. 181–3.

[6] Wood, *Discoveries at Ephesus*, pp. 15–16.

[7] Wood, *Discoveries at Ephesus*, p. 185.

[8] Wood, *Discoveries at Ephesus*, p. 199.

[9] Wood, *Discoveries at Ephesus*, p. 226.

hundred'.[10] Wood was also assisted by three Royal Engineer sappers[11] and the marines of HM Ships (see below).

* * *

The British government funded the entire eleven-year procurement operation at Ephesus. This was confirmed by Spencer Walpole, a member of parliament and trustee of the British Museum, appointed a trustee specifically to represent the museum's interests in the House of Commons. This was important because the Commons was in control of voting funds for museum excavations.

In 1872, Walpole gave a financial breakdown of the costs of the excavations at Ephesus, which he stated 'were begun nearly eight years ago':

> The expenses incurred in the first excavations were comparatively moderate – about £3,000 in four years … the expenses … to [1871] amounted to no less than £8,000 … Mr. Wood estimated … £3,000 to be expended this year, and £3,000 in 1873. They [trustees] immediately applied to the Treasury and the Chancellor of the Exchequer [a trustee], who took the greatest possible interest in these excavations, stated in reply, his readiness to grant by Supplementary estimate £3,000 this year and £3,000 the next.[12]

Wood claimed that 'the total cost of the excavations from first to last was £16,000'.[13]

The excavations were expensive because the trustees 'ordered' Wood to buy all the land needed for excavations to avoid difficulties with obtaining permissions to excavate from landowners.[14]

* * *

The trustees micromanaged the excavations at Ephesus. Wood sent them progress reports *every month* and when anything

---

[10] Wood, *Discoveries at Ephesus*, p. 246.

[11] Wood, *Discoveries at Ephesus*, p. 194.

[12] Spencer Walpole, HC Deb, 3 August 1872, vol. 213, col. 398–439.

[13] Wood, *Discoveries at Ephesus*, p. v.

[14] Letter from Robert W. Cumberbatch to E. P. Barron, 7 May 1870. TNA, FO 198/942, p. 137.

required immediate notice.[15] The trustees sent Newton to
Ephesus four times to monitor excavations – in April 1868,
January 1871, January 1872 and January 1874.[16]

The museum sent Wood stone-cutting saws. He wrote, under
the heading 'Sawing marble', that when he received the saws

> I at once proceeded to make the best use I could, by
> sawing off slabs from bulky stones ... I thus secured all
> that was worth sending, and considerably reduced the
> cost of their transport to England both in the number
> and sizes of the cases, and the amount of freight.[17]

The 462 inscriptions Wood sent to the museum were sawed
from one of the most important classical sites in the world
– one of the Seven Wonders of the Ancient World. This is
staggering.

But there was more. The remains of the Temple of Diana
were mutilated not only with saws but with gunpowder. Wood,
assisted by Royal Engineers, used gunpowder at Ephesus:

> In doing this [excavating foundation-piers of the temple],
> which we partly effected by the aid of gunpowder ...'[18]

In researching this book, this is the only documented record of
the use of gunpowder at an ancient site.

The Admiralty transported the marble from Ephesus to the
British Museum.

In 1871 the Secretary of the museum wrote to the Admiralty
that Wood had for some time been 'employed by the trustees,
excavating the site of the Temple of Diana at Ephesus'.[19] The
Secretary enclosed a request from Newton (now a keeper at the
museum) that the Admiralty provide Wood with the services of
the crew of an HM Ship to haul, pack and load heavy marbles.[20]

---

[15] Wood, *Discoveries at Ephesus*, p. 247.

[16] Wood, *Discoveries at Ephesus*, pp. 162, 176, 195, 255.

[17] Wood, *Discoveries at Ephesus*, p. 206.

[18] Wood, *Discoveries at Ephesus*, p. 259.

[19] Letter from J. Winter Jones to The Right Honourable The Lords Commissioners
of The Admiralty letter, 17 November 1871, Admiralty correspondence 1871. TNA,
ADM 1/6196.

[20] Letter from C. T. Newton to J. Winter Jones, 15 November 1871, Admiralty
correspondence 1871. TNA, ADM 1/6196.

The Admiralty provided Wood, at different times, with twenty marines and four carpenters from HMS *Caledonia*,[21] twenty-two men from HMS *Terrible*,[22] and sixteen from HMS *Antelope*.[23]

The marble was hauled overland from Ephesus to Smyrna, the nearest port. One of the blocks 'weighing upwards of 11 tons, is part of a drum ... mentioned by Pliny'.[24] Wood wrote that HM Ships took 'between 50 and 60 tons of sculptured stones and inscriptions'.[25]

From Smyrna, the Admiralty transported the marble in HM Ships *Antelope, Ariadne, Swiftsure, Terrible* and *Caledonia* (see Appendix 1 for dates, and Appendix 4, an extract from HMS *Caledonia*'s log book). HMS *Terrible*'s log book records, 27 March 1868 at Portsmouth, 'Employed hoisting out ... antiquities for British Museum'.[26] The Digest records 'Men of *Terrible* employed at Ephesus' and 'Antiquities excavated at Ephesus. Thanks of British Museum for services of Capt. Cromwell of *Terrible*'.[27]

Wood wrote, 'In May 1863, having obtained a firman from the Turkish government, through the influence of the trustees of the British Museum, I commenced my excavations at Ephesus'.[28] Wood received annual permissions but endured frustrating periods when there was no permission. He wrote of difficulties renewing annual permissions.

He began excavating in 1863, but in 1872, after nine years at Ephesus, he admitted his excavations were kept *secret*: 'As it was no longer considered necessary to keep our operations secret from the general public, I sent a short account of my discoveries to *The Times*'.[29]

In 1888, the British Museum's introduction to the Ephesus Room claimed that the antiquities had been obtained by Wood at excavations 'during the years 1869–1874'.[30] But Wood wrote he began in 1863 not in 1869.

---

[21] Wood, *Discoveries at Ephesus*, p. 192.

[22] Wood, *Discoveries at Ephesus*, p. 82.

[23] Wood, *Discoveries at Ephesus*, p. 225.

[24] 'The Temple of Diana at Ephesus', *The Times*, 15 February 1872, p. 6.

[25] Wood, *Discoveries at Ephesus*, pp. 225–6.

[26] *Terrible* Ship's Log. TNA, ADM 53/9346.

[27] Admiralty Digest 1868, Case 90a British Museum. TNA, ADM 12/817.

[28] Wood, *Discoveries at Ephesus*, p. 16.

[29] He sent his account on 4 March 1872 (Wood, *Discoveries at Ephesus*, p. 199).

[30] *A Guide to the Exhibition galleries of the British Museum, Bloomsbury* (London: Printed By order of the Trustees, 1888), p. 15.

The fact that it was necessary to keep operations conducted by the trustees secret for nine years (according to Wood) suggests that the Turkish government may not have been fully aware of the duration or the extent of Wood's excavations.

Wood maintained that HMS *Antelope* transported cases of marble from Ephesus in 1873.[31] *Antelope* transported the cases five years earlier, in 1869.[32] He claimed that he arranged for a merchant ship to transport 'twenty-three cases and 63 loose [marble] blocks'.[33] In fact, the twenty-three cases and 63 loose blocks were transported in 1874 by HMS *Revenge* (see Appendix 2). He also claimed that HMS *Ariadne* transported cases in 1873, but Admiralty records established she did not. Wood clearly had something to hide. It can only be that his excavations were not entirely covered by permissions from the Turkish government.

This would explain why the British Museum omitted the first six years of Wood's excavations. It would also explain why the museum distanced itself from the excavations. British Museum Accounts for 1884–85 state that the marbles obtained by Mr. J. T. Wood from Ephesus in 1883 were *donated* to the British Museum 'by the Committee of the Ephesus Exploration Fund, through Mr. Hayter Lewis'.[34] Wood's excavations at Ephesus, which began in 1863 and lasted over a decade, are extensively cited in Foreign Office, Treasury and Admiralty records, but none of the sources mention the Ephesus Exploration Fund or Hayter Lewis.

* * *

As explained in Chapter 9 on Priene, the Museum of Archaeology, Istanbul, displayed a chronological 'History of Research'. The following are *sequential* entries:

> 1842/1843 – C. Texier; first excavations at Magnesia [now Ortaklar, nine miles south-east of Ephesus] etc.
>
> 1891/1893 – C. Humann; starts excavations again etc.

Between the above dates there should be a record of the eleven-year excavations at Ephesus (1863–1874) by John Turtle Wood

---

[31] Wood, *Discoveries at Ephesus*, p. 225.

[32] Case 90a, British Museum. TNA, ADM 12/835, and ADM 53/9633.

[33] Wood, *Discoveries at Ephesus*, p. 284.

[34] Accounts of the British Museum 1884–85. UK PP, paper no. 261, p. 34.

under the directions of the trustees of the British Museum. It should state that over sixty tons of marble was taken from the Temple of Diana to the British Museum. But seemingly the Museum of Archaeology in Istanbul has no record of Wood's excavations.

* * *

The Ephesus Room, at the British Museum in 1888, has been long closed.

In 2012, a display label (in Room 13) informed visitors that 'more sculpture from Ephesus may be seen in Rooms 77, 81 and 82'. However, in 2012, museum attendants explained that Rooms 81 and 82 had been 'closed for many years' (the rooms were no longer shown on the museum's handout floor plan). Despite this, the notice still remains in Room 13 in 2019.[35]

In 2012, there were just *three* of the 462 inscriptions sawed from the Temple of Diana on public display in a small basement, Room 78 (Classical Inscriptions). But this room, too, has been closed and is no longer on the museum floor plan.

In 2019, artefacts from Ephesus on public display are: a sculptured marble drum (Room 22), a marble inscription, and a panel from a Roman mosaic (both Room 70). With these exceptions, the sixty tons of antiquities taken from Ephesus is kept in the British Museum stores.

* * *

With permission or not, the trustees of the British Museum committed a barbaric act in taking over sixty tons of marble from one of the Seven Wonders of the Ancient World. How has this been recorded and reported by historians and writers?

The first history of the British Museum (published 1870) candidly states that the marbles from Ephesus were 'Excavated, at the charge of the Trustees, by Vice-Consul Wood'.[36] (Wood was never a consular official.)

The British Museum: A History (Wilson) has a single sentence on Wood and Ephesus: 'The Museum funded J. T. Wood's excavations at Ephesus'.[37] In fact, the British government

---

[35] Caption photographed 14 February 2019.

[36] Edwards, *Lives of The Founders of the British Museum*, p. 43.

[37] Wilson, *The British Museum*, p. 150.

funded British Museum excavations at Ephesus over eleven years, and they were conducted by J. T. Wood under direction of the trustees.

Wood's entry in the *Oxford Dictionary of National Biography* states he discovered the Temple of Diana at Ephesus, which 'was a sad ruin, but Wood managed to recover a quantity of very broken sculptures and architectural features, which he sent back to Britain'.[38] Clearly this entry needs to be rewritten.

Archaeologists & Aesthetes in the Sculpture galleries of the British Museum 1800–1939 (Ian Jenkins) names Wood as one of the 'extraordinary individuals' who made contributions to the museum collections, but adds nothing more than that the marble he took from the Temple of Diana added to the British Museum's problem of lack of space.[39]

Keeping their Marbles (Tiffany Jenkins) does not mention the Temple of Diana at Ephesus or Wood at all.

* * *

The Temple of Diana at Ephesus, one of the Seven Wonders of the Ancient World, has not acquired the status of a UNESCO World Heritage Site. This is because the site is marked by a *single* column constructed of dissociated marble fragments discovered scattered about Ephesus. The column is unauthentic so does not rate as a UNESCO World Heritage Site.

* * *

In British Museum Accounts (2015–16), it is celebrated that 'the Greek collection includes … elements of two of the Seven Wonders of the Ancient World: the Mausoleum at Halicarnassus and the Temple of Artemis at Ephesos'.[40] The eighty tons of marble taken from Halicarnassus and the sixty tons taken from Ephesus boil down to 'elements'.

---

[38] *Oxford Dictionary of National Biography* Online. Last accessed 24 May 2018.
[39] Ian Jenkins, *Archaeologists & Aesthetes*, p. 212.
[40] British Museum Account 2015–2016. UK PP, HC 249, p. 54.

CHAPTER 12

Rhodes and Bodrum:
Alfred Biliotti, British Consul

In 1861, Alfred Biliotti was appointed British Vice-Consul to Rhodes, which at the time was under Turkish control. Biliotti excavated on Rhodes under the direction of the trustees of the British Museum.

British Museum Accounts for the year ended March 1861 state that Biliotti obtained

> from the cemetery of the ancient town of Cumirus [Cameiros] in Rhodes ... gold ornaments, painted vases, vessels of glass and porcelain, bronzes, and terracottas, remarkable for their preservation and their Archaic character ... a *pinax* or plate, on which is represented the combat of Hector and Menelaus over the body of Euphorbus. The names of the combatants are inscribed over them in very ancient characters.[1]

In order to obtain what he did, 'nearly three hundred tombs were opened'.[2] In 1898, the Keeper of Greek and Roman Antiquities wrote that Biliotti kept no records between 1861 and 1864.

> Unfortunately we possess no similar records of previous acquisitions. We are told nothing of the finding of the Sarcophagus [of Cameiros] nor of a series of vases ... acquired previous to 1864.[3]

---

[1] Acquisitions Schedule to the British Museum's Accounts for the year ended 31 March 1861, HC PP 1861 [220], p. 14.

[2] Edwards, *Lives of The Founders of the British Museum*, p. 669.

[3] A. S. Murray, *Terracotta Sarcophagus: Greek and Etruscan in the British Museum* (London: Longmans & Co, 1898), pp. 15–20.

What should have been properly documented on Rhodes has been lost forever.

The Sarcophagus of Cameiros was a six-foot-long terracotta coffin 'with human heads, animals and floral arrangements are painted in brown and crimson on a pale ground';[4] 'The sarcophagus ... is believed [to be] unique of its kind'.[5]

Biliotti was a tomb raider.

His excavations 'were effected at the public charge'.[6] Therefore, British taxpayers funded a British Vice-Consul to rob nearly three hundred tombs – because the trustees of the British Museum directed it.

* * *

The Admiralty recorded the following request from the British Museum:

> Bodrum Expedition. British Museum requests that a Ship may be permitted to call occasionally & render such assistance to Mr. Biliotti as may be required.[7]

In 1859, HMS *Supply* transported cases with objects that Biliotti took from tombs on Rhodes.[8]

In 1864, Panizzi, at the British Museum, asked the Admiralty to transport everything that Biliotti excavated, describing it as *belonging* to the trustees of the museum.[9]

In July 1864, HMS *Chanticleer* transported Biliotti's collection from Rhodes to Malta for transshipment to England.[10] Malta, British until 1964, was a transportation hub and collection point for antiquities from North Africa, Greece and Turkey. As an example of how Malta was used in 1861, the Foreign Office instructed the Vice-Consul at Benghazi 'to send to the care of

---

[4] British Museum Accounts. UK PP, 1864 (246), p. 16.

[5] C.T. Newton, 'Recent Acquisitions in the Department of Greek and Roman Antiquities at the British Museum', *The Fine Arts Quarterly Review*, vol. 1 (May 1863), pp. 191–2.

[6] Edwards, *Lives of The Founders of the British Museum*, p. 669.

[7] Admiralty Digest 1865, Case 90a British Museum. TNA, ADM 12/768.

[8] *Further Papers respecting the Excavations at Budrum and Cnidus: Presented to the House of Lords by Command of Her Majesty. 1859* (London: Harrison and Sons, 1859); UK PP, Series 2 [2575], pp. 99–101.

[9] *Promiscuous* 1864. TNA, ADM 1/5911.

[10] TNA, ADM 53/8459.

the Admiralty at Malta a Sarcophagus for the British Museum & request that directions may be given to send the Sarcophagus to England'.[11]

In 1862, the auctioneers S. Leigh Sotheby & John Williams auctioned a collection of ancient Greek pottery from Cameiros on Rhodes. The preface in the auction catalogue candidly stated, 'The site has been explored for several years under the auspices of the Foreign Office, by Mr. A. Biliotti, British Vice-Consul at Rhodes'.[12]

Biliotti was next appointed Vice-Consul at Bodrum to complete Newton's excavations of the Mausoleum of Halicarnassus. The British Museum Accounts for the years 1865, 1866 and 1867 include expenditure on 'Further excavations at Bodrum, under the superintendence of Mr. Vice-Consul Biliotti' (see Appendix 1).

In April 1865, the Admiralty recorded, 'Bodrum Expedition – British Museum requests that a ship may be permitted to call occasionally & render such assistance to Mr. Biliotti as may be required'. In July 1865, HMS *Orontes* arrived in England with forty-four cases of antiquities from Bodrum.[13] The British Museum acknowledged receipt of them on 20 July 1865.[14]

While Biliotti was at Bodrum he also took 'sculptures from a Doric tomb at Bargylia, in Caria which was similar in character to the Lion Tomb near Cnidus'.[15]

* * *

Biliotti made an important contribution to the British Museum collections (mainly from graves on Rhodes and excavations at Bodrum), but he has been buried by the British Museum.

Biliotti is not mentioned in *The British Museum: A History*. Wilson's book states that the collection from Rhodes was brought to England by Robert Murdoch Smith, described as the Captain

---

[11] Admiralty Digest 1860, Case 90a British Museum. TNA, ADM 12/689.
[12] 'Ancient Greek Pottery excavated by Messrs. Biliotti & Salzmann, in the necropolis of Camirus, Island of Rhodes', Lugt number 26784, S. Leigh Sotheby & John Williams catalogue, 10 May 1862, Preface, n.p.
[13] Admiralty Digest 1865, Case 90a British Museum. TNA, ADM 12/768.
[14] Admiralty correspondence, 1865. TNA, ADM 1/5958.
[15] Acquisitions Schedule to the British Museum's Accounts for the year ended 31 March 1866, HC PP 1866 (187), p. 19.

of HMS *Gorgon*.[16] Smith was not in the Navy.[17] Smith was a Royal Engineer. He assisted Newton to dismantle the Mausoleum at Halicarnassus, and in the following year he excavated at Cyrene on behalf of the British Museum (see Chapter 13).

Biliotti is not named in the British Museum online provenance database, despite being named by the museum in 1876 as the finder of two important sculptures at Halicarnassus – a 'Circular Altar, encircled with a frieze representing the nine Muses' and 'Fragment of a Female Tern'.[18]

Biliotti is not named in the *Catalogue of the Jewellery, Greek Etruscan and Roman in the Department of Antiquities, British Museum*, which has 108 objects 'from excavations at Kameiros, Rhodes' where Biliotti opened the tombs.[19]

And Biliotti is not named in *Keeping their Marbles* (Tiffany Jenkins).

* * *

It is *impossible* to erase Consul Alfred Biliotti's contribution to the British Museum. This is because what he took, under direction of the trustees, is described in British Museum Accounts for the years 1861, 1862, 1864, 1865, 1866, 1867–68 and 1868–69. The accounts, presented to parliament, state that Biliotti excavated 'on account of the trustees' and 'under the direction of the trustees of the British Museum'.

---

[16] Wilson, *The British Museum*, p. 125.

[17] C. T. Bedford was Captain of *Gorgon* (*The Navy List*, London: John Murray, 1856).

[18] *Synopsis of the Contents of the British Museum: Department of Greek and Roman Antiquities: Greco-Roman Sculptures* (London: Printed by Order of the Trustees, 1876), Part II, pp. 35, 59.

[19] F. H. Marshall *Catalogue of the Jewellery, Greek Etruscan and Roman in the Department of Antiquities, British Museum* (First published 1911. Oxford: Oxford University Press, 1969), pp. 85–100.

CHAPTER 13

Cyrene: Lieutenants R. M. Smith, R.E. and E. A. Porcher, R.N.

Cyrene was one of five Greek cities in the coastal region of Cyrenaica (the eastern part of Libya today). Cyrenaica was colonised by the Phoenicians, the Greeks and the Romans.

In 1821, Captain Frederick Beechey (Royal Navy) was sent on an expedition to the north coast of Africa and wrote a book that contained two chapters on Cyrene.[1] His book has a plan of Cyrene and six illustrated panoramic plates of the city which include: Position of the Amphitheatre, the Fountain of Apollo, Entrance to the Fountain, Tombs on the Heights of Cyrene, and other views of Cyrene.[2]

Beechey wrote, 'there are still many statues above ground, in excellent style. One of these, from ... the armour, is probably a statue of one of the Ptolemies; and near it is a female statue, one of the Cleopatras, Berenices or Arsinoës'.[3] He described 'sculptured three female figures, joining hands as if performing a sacred dance ... beautiful bas-relief of white marble ... the torso of a male figure the size of life (also of white marble) executed in the best style of Grecian sculpture'.[4]

Beechey did not take any antiquities.

Cyrene was a granary of Greek and Roman antiquities and an obvious target for the trustees of the British Museum.

---

[1] Captain F. W. Beechey, et al. *Proceedings of the Expedition to explore the Northern Coast of Africa, from Tripoli eastward; in 1821 and 1822* (London: John Murray, 1828).

[2] Beechey, *Proceedings of the Expedition to explore the Northern Coast of Africa*, Plates 9–14.

[3] Beechey, *Proceedings of the Expedition to explore the Northern Coast of Africa*, p. 527.

[4] Beechey, *Proceedings of the Expedition to explore the Northern Coast of Africa*, pp. 426, 433.

In 1860, forty years after Captain Beechey, Lieutenant Robert Murdoch Smith (Royal Engineer) and Lieutenant Edwin A. Porcher (Royal Navy) were sent to Cyrene on an expedition under the auspices of the British government. They state this in the full title of their co-authored book, *History of the Recent Discoveries at Cyrene made during an Expedition to the Cyrenaica in 1860–61, under the Auspices of Her Majesty's Government.*[5]

They claimed their expedition was under government auspices, but Newton (Keeper at the British Museum) said elsewhere that the 'explorations were carried on under the direction of the Trustees of the British Museum'.[6] Smith and Porcher wrote, 'The trustees of the British Museum [had] given us authority to draw bills on them to the amount of £500'.[7]

Therefore, Cyrene is another prime example of where the line between the government and the trustees is blurred when it comes to taking antiquities for the British Museum.

* * *

In Chapter 1 of this book, the 'large torso in armour' described by Beechey in 1821 was given as an example of how the trustees used the works of early explorers to pinpoint antiquities. Smith and Porcher secured that very sculpture.[8] In fact, they took 148 sculptures (described in their 'List of Sculptures Found on various sites at Cyrene') and thirty-three inscriptions (listed in 'Inscriptions discovered or found at Cyrene with translations').[9]

The sculptures taken included: The Nymph of Cyrene overcoming a Lion; Jupiter Ammon; Group of Venus and Cupid; Aegipan; Isis; Minerva (Athena); Iconic Statue of a Young Girl; The Panther of Bacchus; Venus (Aphrodite); Relief, Cyrene crowned by Libya; Head of Lucius Verus; and Head of one of the Dioscuri.[10]

---

[5] Robert Murdoch Smith, R.E., and Edwin Augustus Porcher, R.N. *History of the Recent Discoveries at Cyrene made during an Expedition to the Cyrenaica in 1860–61, under the Auspices of Her Majesty's Government* (London: Day, 1864).

[6] Newton, ed., *The Collection of Ancient Greek Inscriptions in the British Museum*, Part I, Preface, n.p.

[7] Smith and Porcher, *History of the Recent Discoveries at Cyrene*, p. 73.

[8] 'Further Discoveries at Cyrene', *The Times*, 29 October 1861, p. 8.

[9] Smith and Porcher, *History of the Recent Discoveries at Cyrene*, pp. 99–117.

[10] *Synopsis of the Contents of the British Museum: Department of Greek and Roman Antiquities: Greco-Roman Sculptures* (London: Printed by Order of the Trustees, 1876), Part II.

In November 1861, *The Illustrated London News* included engravings of five of the museum's statues from Cyrene and credited the Foreign Office for obtaining them.[11]

* * *

How did two junior officers in the British Army and Navy come to take antiquities from North Africa? The contention here is that the idea for the expedition originated at the British Museum. However, in order to distance the museum from its role in instigating the expedition, Newton dressed it up as being Smith's idea.

The following is how the expedition, under the auspices of the government, came to be sent to Cyrene.

In 1859, Smith helped Newton to dismantle the Mausoleum at Halicarnassus (see Chapter 8). In May 1860, Smith wrote to General Sir John Burgoyne at the War Office to propose 'a small exploring & surveying expedition' to North Africa and, in particular, to Cyrene.[12] The contention here is that Newton prepared Smith's submission.

Smith drew Burgoyne's attention to Beechey's book, quoting passages from Cyrene: 'I would especially call your attention to the following passage at p. 527. There are several other statues above ground in this part of the city'. Smith offered to make 'a report on the feasibility of the expedition for the purpose of removing some of the sculptures'. He added that he had written to Newton 'to bring the proposal under the notice of the trustees of the British Museum'.[13] Smith was a Royal Engineer and unlikely to be conversant with Beechey's book. Newton, as Keeper at the British Museum, knew it intimately and fed passages to Smith.

Newton promptly wrote to Burgoyne, pressing him to back Smith's proposal and advising that 'Cyrenaica ... the site of the celebrated Pentapolis of Greek cities, is a district *full of antiquities* ... [and] one of the most promising for archaeological discovery in the whole Mediterranean' [emphasis added].[14]

---

[11] 'The Cyrene Marbles in the British Museum', *The Illustrated London News*, 30 November 1861, pp. 563–4.

[12] Letter from R. M. Smith to General Sir J Burgoyne, 18 May 1860, Admiralty correspondence 1860. TNA, ADM 1/5745.

[13] Letter from R. M. Smith to General Sir J Burgoyne, 18 May 1860, Admiralty correspondence 1860. TNA, ADM 1/5745.

[14] Letter from C. T. Newton to General Sir J Burgoyne, 29 May 1860, Admiralty correspondence 1860. TNA, ADM 1/5745.

Burgoyne requested assistance from E. Hammond (Foreign Office) who, as directed by Lord John Russell (Foreign Secretary and trustee of the British Museum), alerted William G. Romaine at the Admiralty. Meanwhile, Panizzi (British Museum), also quoting from Beechey's book, wrote to the Duke of Somerset (First Lord of the Admiralty and trustee of the British Museum) to ask that the Commander in Chief of the Mediterranean Fleet give Smith and Porcher 'all assistance in his power'. The commander did and the two British officers were transported to North Africa to take antiquities for the British Museum.

The Foreign Office advised Major G. F. Herman, Consul-General at Tripoli, that the two would be coming.[15] The Consul-General advised F. H. Crowe, the Vice-Consul at Benghazi, that Smith and Porcher 'are about to *explore* the district called the "Cyrenaica" and I have to instruct you to take any steps in your power to promote the *Exploration Expedition*' [emphasis added].[16]

The government funded the eleven-month expedition. British Museum Accounts record expenditure on 'Excavations in the Cyrenaica under Lieutenant Smith R.E. and Porcher R.N. and removal of Antiquities to the Museum'.[17]

The Admiralty received a request: 'Trustees of the British Museum for a ship to be sent to ... Cyrene, to assist in researches after antiquities etc., conducted by Lieutenant Smith R.E., and Lieutenant Porcher, R.N.'.[18]

The Admiralty sent two ships and charged the British Museum for 'Cyrene Expedition: Claim for supply of provisions & seamen's clothing supplied from the [HMS] *Scourge* & [HMS] *Melpomene* ... to be made on British Museum'.[19]

An entry in HMS *Melpomene*'s log book highlights the number of men involved in taking antiquities: 'Party left the ship for Cyrene. Consisting of 94 Seamen & 33 Mariners'.[20] Smith and Porcher could have achieved little on their own. In

---

[15] Letter from Foreign Office to Major G. F. Herman, 18 July 1860. TNA, FO 160/78.

[16] Letter from Major G. F. Herman to F. H. Crowe, 18 July 1860. TNA, FO 101/47.

[17] British Museum Accounts, 31 March 1862, UK PP, 1861–1862 (200), p. 3.

[18] Navy: Return of Applications by Commercial Interests for Ships of War, 1862. UK PP, paper no. 380, p. 5.

[19] Case 90a British Museum. TNA, ADM 12/736.

[20] TNA, ADM 53/7575.

their book, Smith and Porcher thanked 'the officers and crew of the *Assurance* and *Melpomene* who cheerfully and efficiently carried out the orders of the Admiralty in the removal of the sculpture from Cyrene [twelve miles from the coast] to the place of embarkation'.[21] The Admiralty recouped from the 'Trustees of British Museum ... the Pay of Men employed transporting Statuary from Cyrene'.[22]

* * *

General Burgoyne (War Office) wrote to Hammond (Treasury):

> Lieutenant R. M. Smith R.E. [was] proposing an exploration excursion on the coast of N. Africa, to the district of which Cyrene was anciently the chief city ... he would limit his proceedings to observations & reports, & not attempt excavations nor removal of objects of interest *without a distinct permission* [emphasis added].[23]

Smith was fresh from assisting Newton with taking 385 cases of antiquities from Bodrum. There can be no doubting his real intentions for going to Cyrene. Smith and Porcher did not have permission to take antiquities from Cyrene but claimed they did. The 'exploration expedition' was a cover for a covert excavation operation.

Smith and Porcher went to Cyrene, departing from Malta for Tripoli by HMS *Boxer* on 19 November 1860. They claimed that having arrived in Tripoli on 21 November 1860 they met Colonel Herman, Consul-General in Tripoli, who had already obtained the firman (permission) from the Pasha or Governor of Barbary: 'Having found on our arrival at Tripoli that our firman gave us authority to dig for sculptures, and remove such as we found'.[24] There are four untruths in what they claim.

They did sail from Malta on 19 November 1860, but not to Tripoli. HMS *Boxer* took them to Benghazi where they arrived on 30 November 1860. HMS *Boxer*'s log book records

---

[21] Smith and Porcher, *History of the Recent Discoveries at Cyrene*, Preface, n.p.

[22] Naval Receipt and Expenditure for Naval Services year ended 1862. UK PP, paper no. 387, p.20.

[23] Letter from General Sir J Burgoyne to E. Hammond, 7 June 1860, TNA, ADM 1/5745.

[24] Smith and Porcher, *History of the Recent Discoveries at Cyrene*, p. 23.

them boarding and disembarking.[25] In Benghazi they were met by Frederick H. Crowe, the Vice-Consul, who wrote to Herman in Tripoli notifying him that Smith and Porcher had arrived.[26] Within a week, Smith and Porcher left Benghazi for Cyrene and Crowe advised Herman of this. Therefore, Smith and Porcher did not meet Herman and he never gave them a firman. Furthermore, Herman was never instructed by the Foreign Office to obtain a permission. Herman advised Crowe that Smith and Porcher were coming on an 'Exploring Expedition'. This is what the Foreign Office advised Herman. An exploring expedition is very different from an excavating expedition. The Foreign Office never asked Herman to obtain a permission for Smith and Porcher to excavate or remove any antiquities.

Smith and Porcher were not telling the truth when they claimed they had permission 'to dig for sculptures, and remove such as we found'. The significant thing here is that the trustees of the British Museum and the government *knew* that no permission had been granted, yet they funded and sent Smith and Porcher to take antiquities.

* * *

It appears to have been the norm to take antiquities from North Africa without permission. Two months before Smith and Porcher arrived, Crowe, the Vice-Consul at Benghazi, wrote to Lord Russell to say he had excavated, among other objects, eight sarcophagi, three of white marble and five of stone, and if they were of interest to the British Museum the objects were 'entirely at the disposal of Her Majesty's Government'.[27] This was not conditional on obtaining permission. Russell replied that the trustees wanted everything.[28] Crowe was subsequently advised by the Foreign Office that Russell authorised him 'to draw a Bill upon his Lordship' for his expenses in obtaining the antiquities, adding 'you will <u>not</u> include this Bill or the charges to which it is applied in your accounts with the Treasury' [Russell's

---

[25] HMS *Boxer* Ship's Log, May 1860–March 1861, TNA, ADM 53/7101.
[26] Letter from F. H. Crowe to Herman, 3 December 1860. TNA, FO 160/78.
[27] Letter from F. H. Crowe to Lord Russell, 1 September 1860. TNA, FO 101/47.
[28] Letter from Lord Russell to F. H. Crowe, 21 November 1860. TNA, FO 101/47.

emphasis].[29] In other words, the expenditure on obtaining the antiquities was not to appear in public accounts.

Two of the white marble sarcophagi and 'several fine terracotta figures and lamps and fragments of a statuette in gypsum ... obtained for the museum by the late F. H. Crowe, Her Majesty's Consul' entered the museum's collections in 1862.[30]

* * *

Panizzi, at the museum, asked the Admiralty to waste no time in taking the statues from Cyrene found by Smith and Porcher, claiming 'if they remain exposed, [they] run the risk of mutilation at the hands of the fanatical Arabs of the district'.[31] However, the 'many statues above ground' described by Beechey in 1821 had been left well alone for centuries, as had ones in an illustration captioned 'A tomb embellished with figures' in Smith and Porcher's book.[32] There was no new or imminent threat. The very real and actual danger to the statues was not from the locals but from fanatics in Bloomsbury. If this is doubted, Panizzi sent the Admiralty a 'Schedule of Stores for the use of Lieutenants Smith & Porcher at Cyrene' and it included:

> Stone saws............................... Nos. 2.
> And Mason's grit for the use of them.[33]

The above mentioned tomb, embellished with figures, was one of many mutilated using Panizzi's saws. The figures will be among the 148 'Sculptures Found on various sites at Cyrene'. Today the sculptures are buried in British Museum stores, together with the thirty-three inscriptions sawed from marble blocks, devastating temples and buildings at Cyrene.

* * *

Tiffany Jenkins' book *Keeping their Marbles* does not mention Cyrene, Smith, Porcher or the 148 marble sculptures they took

---

[29] Letter from Foreign Office to F. H. Crowe, 1 April 1861. TNA, FO 101/48.

[30] British Museum Accounts, 31 March 1862. UK PP, 1862 (200), p. 17.

[31] Letter from Antonio Panizzi to Duke of Somerset, 16 March 1861, Admiralty: Miscellaneous; British Museum 1861. TNA, ADM 1/5777.

[32] Smith and Porcher, *History of the Recent Discoveries at Cyrene*, Plate 19.

[33] Letter from Antonio Panizzi to Duke of Somerset, 30 July 1861, Admiralty: Miscellaneous; British Museum 1861. TNA, ADM 1/5777.

under the auspices of the British government (according to Smith and Porcher) and the directions of the trustees of the British Museum (according to Newton).[34]

Smith's and Porcher's biographical details in the British Museum online collection database (2019) are neither accurate nor complete.

Robert Murdoch Smith's biography states:

- that he was an 'archaeologist: military/naval'. Not true. Smith was not in the Navy, he was a Royal Engineer. This is known at the British Museum. In Room 70 there are five Roman statues with the caption, 'From Cyrene, North Africa … Found by Lieutenant R. M. Smith, RE, [Royal Engineer] and Commander E. A. Porcher, RN [Royal Navy]';[35]
- that he 'excavated at Halicarnassus, Cnidus and Cyrene'. The fact he excavated at all three sites under directions of the trustees of the museum and funded by the government is not mentioned; and
- that he was 'author of *Persian Art* (London 1876)'. He was, but his *History of the Recent Discoveries at Cyrene … under the Auspices of Her Majesty's Government* is not mentioned.

Edwin A. Porcher's biography states:

- that he was an 'archaeologist: military/naval'. Correct;
- that he 'was involved in the exploration of Cyrene'. In fact, he explored, drew, sawed and took antiquities. It is not mentioned that he assisted Davis at Carthage (see Chapter 14). Porcher drew antiquities for the trustees. Newton wrote, 'I have seen some drawings made by Lieut. Porcher in the district of Carthage';[36] and
- that he was author of *By Seaways to Cyrene*. His co-authored book with Smith is not mentioned.

* * *

---

[34] Tiffany Jenkins, *Keeping their Marbles*.

[35] BM Room 70 Roman Empire; captions photographed 15 February 2019.

[36] Letter from C. T. Newton to General Sir J Burgoyne, 29 May 1860, Admiralty correspondence 1860, NA ADM 1/5745.

In the preface to their book they thank 'the Government authorities and the Trustees of the British Museum [and] Mr. C. T. Newton'.[37]

There may be a number of reasons why the British Museum does not mention their book. One is that the museum has disassociated Smith and Porcher from some of the sculptures they took from Cyrene. For example, the massive 'Marble statue of Apollo holding a kithera' from Cyrene that is exhibited in the museum[38] is 'Apollo Citharoedus' photographed in Smith and Porcher's book.[39] Smith and Porcher are not mentioned in the display label.

They also took the 'Bronze head of a north African'[40] and 'Marble head of a Ptoematic ruler'[41] on display at the museum. These are photographed in their book, but again Smith and Porcher are not mentioned in the museum display label.

The British Museum does name Smith and Porcher in the provenance of five statues from Cyrene in Room 70, but clearly the museum is intent on downplaying their contribution to the museum collections. The problem with their book is that it exposes the whole truth – with one exception, which is revealed in Chapter 23 (Britain's Best-Kept Secret).

---

[37] Smith and Porcher, *History of the Recent Discoveries at Cyrene*, Preface, n.p.

[38] BM Room 22, GR. 1861-7-251.

[39] Smith and Porcher, *History of the Recent Discoveries at Cyrene*, Plate 62; the statue photographed on a pedestal in the museum.

[40] BM, GR.1861.11-27.13.

[41] BM, GR.1861.7-25.11.

CHAPTER 14

Carthage: Nathan Davis

The city of Carthage, present-day Tunis, was founded in the ninth century BC.

Between 1856 and 1859, ninety-three cases of Phoenician, Greek and Roman antiquities, which had remained undisturbed for centuries, were taken from Carthage and nearby Utica by Nathan Davis for the British Museum.

He took the following:

- Roman mosaics pavements, which are described in the British Museum Accounts for the years 1858, 1860 and 1861. Twenty-eight of the mosaics were catalogued by the museum in 1876.[1] In 2019, twenty-six mosaics from Carthage and Utica were on display on the museum's West Stairs without any reference to Davis. A further two, with the provenance 'excavated by N. Davis', were in Room 70.[2] On the West Stairs there are also eleven Roman mosaic pavements from Halicarnassus taken by Newton, with another three of his in Room 70;

- Phoenician inscriptions, catalogued by the British Museum in 1863;[3]

---

[1] *Synopsis of the Contents of the British Museum: Department of Greek and Roman Antiquities: Greco-Roman Sculptures* (London: Printed by Order of the Trustees, 1876), pp. 75–88.

[2] BM Room 70; caption photographed 14 February 2019.

[3] *Inscriptions in the Phoenician Character now deposited in the British Museum discovered on the site of Carthage, during researches made by Nathan Davis Esq., at the expense of her Majesty's Government in the years 1856, 1857 and 1858* (London: Printed by Order of the Trustees, 1863).

- marble statues, catalogued by the museum in 1876, the most notable being a torso, probably of a Roman emperor, and the head of Apollo;[4] and
- 'more than 150 limestone funerary stelae, many from the *tophet*, a cemetery at Carthage for the burial of young children.'[5]

Davis was *employed* by the British government in Carthage on the recommendation of the British Museum. This will come as a complete surprise to those who have read any account that explains how the British Museum obtained its Carthaginian antiquities.

In August 1856, the British Museum requested that the Foreign Office accept an offer from Davis to excavate at Carthage and suggested paying him a salary of one guinea per day.[6] The Foreign Secretary engaged Davis in December 1856 with instructions to 'send home' everything he found.[7]

The British government paid for Davis' excavations. This is stated in British Museum Accounts in 1860 and 1861, which record antiquities from Carthage entering the collections: '51 cases from the excavations of the Rev N. Davis at Carthage and Utica ... the result of excavations carried on at the expense of Her Majesty's Government'[8]; and 'A further collection of antiquities, excavated by the Rev. Nathan Davis, at the expense of Her Majesty's Government ... [at] Carthage'.[9]

The government funded excavations at Carthage, but the expenditure was kept out of British Museum Accounts. The accounts record specific parliamentary grants for excavations in Assyria, Bodrum, Cyrene, Ephesus, Xanthus and at other ancient sites (see Appendix 1) – but not at Carthage. To pay for the excavations at Carthage, the British Consul at Tunis drew

---

[4] *Synopsis of the Contents of the British Museum: Department of Greek and Roman Antiquities: Greco-Roman Sculptures* (London: Printed by Order of the Trustees, 1876), p. 37; p. 44.

[5] BM Room B1; caption photographed 14 February 2019.

[6] Letter from A. Panizzi to Earl of Clarendon, 12 August 1856. TNA, FO 78/1334, pp. 42–3.

[7] Letter from E. Hammond to Rev. N. Davis, 31 December 1856. TNA, FO 335/108.

[8] British Museum Accounts, 31 March 1860. UK PP, 1860 (311), pp. 13–15.

[9] British Museum Accounts, 31 March 1861. UK PP, 1861 (220), p. 14.

Bills of Exchange on the Foreign Secretary in favour of Davis.

The Foreign Secretary instructed Davis ('in order to facilitate the auditing of his accounts') to keep a register of the labourers he employed and to send this, together with 'a list of all the objects found', to the British Consul at Tunis every month.[10]

Between December 1856 and December 1859, Davis submitted nine detailed invoices of expenses, which even included the number of nails used. Curiously, every invoice totalled exactly £200.[11]

The Consul reimbursed Davis, and also paid him £96 quarterly, 'being the amount of ... salary as superintendent for the excavations on the site of ancient Carthage'.[12] This is the guinea-a-day rate suggested by the museum.

The title of a book about the Phoenician inscriptions taken by Davis, printed by order of the trustees of the British Museum, includes the words 'During researches made by Nathan Davis Esq., at the expense of Her Majesty's Government in the years 1856, 1857 and 1858'.[13] However, the trustees omitted the year 1859. Although a display label in the museum in 2019 states that 'From 1856 to 1858 Davis was employed by the Museum to undertake excavations at Carthage and Utica, north Africa',[14] Davis actually excavated throughout 1859; his last £200 invoice is dated December 1859.

Twenty-one Bills of Exchange issued by the British Consul in favour of Davis are at The National Archives.[15] Samples have been photographed (as is permitted) because government files transferred to the archives can be withdrawn and revert to being official secrets. This is because files are deemed to be loaned, which means government departments can simply ask for files to be returned. This happened to 26,898 files between 2011 and early 2014.[16]

---

[10] Letter from E. Hammond to Rev. N. Davis, 13 January 1857. TNA, FO 335/108.

[11] TNA, FO 335/110.

[12] Letter from Richard Wood (Consul) to the Earl of Malmesbury, 31 January 1859. TNA, FO 335/110.

[13] *Inscriptions in the Phoenician Character now deposited in the British Museum discovered on the site of Carthage, during researches made by Nathan Davis Esq., at the expense of her Majesty's Government in the years 1856, 1857 and 1858* (London: Printed by Order of the Trustees, 1863).

[14] BM Room B1; caption photographed 14 February 2019.

[15] TNA, FO 335/110.

[16] Ian Cobain, *The History Thieves* (London: Portobello, 2016), p. 147.

Davis himself confirmed that the British government paid for the excavations at Carthage: 'We were still digging at this place ... when I received an intimation from the Foreign Office to stop excavations. Mr. Hammond writing to me by the direction of Lord Malmesbury [Foreign Secretary and Trustee of the British Museum] says that Her Majesty's Government ... do not feel justified in authorizing any further expenditure for that purpose'.[17]

In 1857, the Foreign Secretary advised the Admiralty that Davis was excavating at Carthage 'on account of Her Majesty's Government' and asked the Admiralty to bring back the antiquities he found, adding, 'For obvious reasons it is desirable that this service should be conducted quietly'.[18]

The Admiralty recorded the following from the Foreign Office: 'Excavations on site of ancient Carthage. F.O. requests that one of H.M. Ships should be sent occasionally to Tunis to bring away antiquities';[19] and 'Antiquities from Carthage – Application for conveyance, request from British Museum that antiquities collected by Rev. N. Davis may be conveyed to England in one of H.M. Ships'.[20]

* * *

The antiquities from Carthage were transported to England by the Admiralty in HM Ships *Curacoa, Caradoc, Kertch* and *Supply*, the latter doing so twice.[21] As an example of entries relating to one of the four ships, HMS *Curacoa*'s log records on Wednesday 26 August 1857 at Woolwich says, 'Employed disembarking Mosaics and other antiquities from Carthage'.[22] The Admiralty Digest records that *Curacoa* received thirty-nine cases of antiquities from Carthage.[23]

---

[17] Dr N. Davis, *Carthage and her Remains: Being an account of the excavations and researches on the site of the Phoenician metropolis conducted under the Auspices of Her Majesty's Government* (London: Richard Bentley, 1861), p. 541.

[18] Letter from the Earl of Clarendon to Lords of the Admiralty, 6 February 1857. TNA, FO 335/108.

[19] Admiralty Digest 1857, Case 90a British Museum. TNA, ADM 12/640.

[20] Admiralty Accounts with the Foreign Office, Case 69.1, 1860. TNA, ADM 12/689.

[21] See Appendix 2.

[22] *Curacoa* Ship's Log. TNA, ADM 53/5830.

[23] Admiralty Digest 1857, Case 90a British Museum. TNA, ADM 12/640.

In addition to transporting antiquities, the Admiralty provided marines to excavate them. Davis wrote, 'I employed the fifteen marines of the [HMS] *Harpy* in opening trenches'.[24] Lieutenant E. A. Porcher of the Royal Navy, who excavated with Smith at Cyrene, was sent to assist Davis in Carthage. As stated in the previous chapter, Newton commented on Porcher's drawings in Carthage.

* * *

The excavations at Carthage were kept out of the British Museum Accounts and funded in such a discreet way because, it is asserted here, there was no permission to take all that Davis took from Carthage.

The British Museum put Davis forward to the Foreign Office and he served a useful purpose. Davis claims he obtained the firman (permission) from the Basha of Tunis to take the antiquities, but he never saw the permission, writing that it may have mistakenly been posted to France: 'The permission never reached me ... though every exertion has been made to trace the document, in England and France, all efforts proved fruitless'.[25] Davis made the ludicrous assertion that he turned the French postal system upside down because the permission was given to a Frenchman in Tunis to post, but he may have inadvertently posted it to France.[26]

Even if permission was granted, its extent cannot have been known, as neither Davis nor the Foreign Office (which employed him) or the trustees (who received everything) saw it.

Yet nearly one hundred cases of antiquities were taken. This would explain why the excavations at Carthage were kept out of the British Museum Accounts and why it is now claimed that Davis *personally* donated and/or sold everything from Carthage to the museum.

* * *

Here are the different ways it is claimed the British Museum obtained its antiquities from Carthage, in chronological order.

---

[24] Davis, *Carthage and her Remains*, p. 510.

[25] Davis, *Carthage and her Remains*, p. 47.

[26] Davis, *Carthage and her Remains*, p. 47.

In 1861 Davis, calling himself Dr Davis, wrote a book in which he claimed he gave the antiquities to the museum.[27] But given the Foreign Office employed him as superintendent, none of the antiquities were his to give.

In 1870, the first history of the museum claimed that 'the Carthaginian Antiquities ... excavated (partly at the cost of the trustees) by Nathan Davis ... [were] purchased from the Collector'.[28] There are two errors here. The first is the implication that Davis paid the balance of what the trustees paid. However, neither Davis nor the trustees paid anything; the government paid everything. The second error is that Davis did not sell anything to the museum because nothing belonged to him.

In 2002, *The British Museum: A History* (Wilson) ducked the issue by devoting a single sentence to Carthage and Davis. It is claimed that the museum did not have space for the 'new finds' excavated by Davis at Carthage.[29] Therefore, the most authoritative history of the museum gives no indication as to what Davis' 'finds' were. It does not mention the floor-to-ceiling Roman mosaics on the museum's West Stairs.

The Oxford Dictionary of National Biography states that, in 1852, the 'Reverend Nathan Davis' was the editor of the *Hebrew Christian Magazine* and he donated everything from Carthage to the museum (not true), adding that his donations were particularly appreciated by the British Museum 'because he was an American'.[30]

In 2016, *Keeping their Marbles* (Tiffany Jenkins) does not mention the Roman marble statues and mosaics taken from Carthage.

In 2019, the British Museum collection online database states that Davis 'excavated on behalf of the British Museum at Carthage and Utica often in association with the British Consul-General Sir Thomas Reade.'[31] The entry is a tacit acknowledgement that Davis did not donate or sell anything to the British Museum.

---

[27] Davis, *Carthage and her Remains*, p. 47.

[28] Edward Edwards, *Lives of the Founders of the British Museum* (London: Trübner, 1870), p. 39.

[29] David M. Wilson, *The British Museum: A History* (London: The British Museum Press, 2002), p. 125.

[30] *Oxford Dictionary of National Biography* (*ODNB*) <http://www.oxforddnb.com>. Accessed 11 March 2019.

[31] British Museum online database. Accessed 11 March 2019.

Nathan Davis should not be grouped with 'the enterprise of a few extraordinary individuals' who made contributions to the museum collections.[32] He was a front for covert British Museum excavations in Cyrene funded by the government.

---

[32] Jenkins, *Keeping their Marbles*, pp. 13–14.

CHAPTER 15

Xanthus: Charles Fellows

In 1838, Charles Fellows, an English explorer, was the first European to discover Xanthus, the capital of ancient Lycia in south-west Turkey.

In 1843–4 eighty tons of marble, packed in eighty-two cases, was taken from Xanthus to the British Museum. Fellows played a role in taking the marble, but it is *not* the lead role that is ascribed to him today. His alleged role is a cover-up, intended to distance the trustees of the British Museum and the British government from having any involvement in taking the marble.

Fellows' role was *minimal.*

* * *

The marbles taken from Xanthus include: the Nereid Monument (390–380 BC) that today dominates Room 17 of the museum; the Payava Tomb (360 BC); the Lion Tomb (600–575 BC); the Tomb of Kybernis, King of Xanthus, known as the 'Harpy Tomb' (480 BC); and the Tomb of Merehi (390–350 BC). These are collectively known as the 'Xanthian Marbles'.

A display panel in Room 17 refers to the Harpy Tomb in Room 15 and the Payava Tomb in Room 20. The monumental Tomb of Merehi from Xanthus is not mentioned. In 2019, it is on display in Room 20a, 'Greek Vases'.

The British Museum, and others, make five claims relating to Fellows: that he paid out of his own resources to take the Xanthian Marbles; that he had a team in Xanthus; that he conducted operations at Xanthus; that he excavated at Xanthus; and that he transported the Xanthian Marbles to England.

There is not an iota of truth in *any one* of the five claims. The fictitious claims are a clear indication that either there was no Turkish government permission or, if there was any, its scope did not extend to taking the Xanthian Marbles.

* * *

Fellows did not pay anything to take the Xanthian Marbles. The British government paid all the costs.

The true cost of obtaining the Xanthus Marbles was not made public. The total cost, in the British Museum Accounts up to 1846, is £3,764. However, in July 1845 the Treasury recorded in correspondence with the British Museum, 'Credit for £6,217 for expenses of the Xanthian Antiquities'.[1] British Museum Accounts and Treasury records, spanning four years, include expenditure, totalling £10,972, that relates to taking and transporting the Xanthian Marbles (see Appendix 1).

Fellows claimed that his expenses in Turkey 'did not exceed £70', which he spent on tools and hiring cattle.[2] He confirmed that he was fully reimbursed by a resolution of the trustees of the museum passed on 14 May 1842.[3] Therefore, Fellows paid nothing. But the *Oxford Dictionary of National Biography* claims 'it was his money ... which made the expedition a success ... He spent considerable sums of his own money to ensure that antiquities were carefully removed and transported'.[4]

The British Museum: A History describes Fellows as 'a rich amateur'.[5] He may well have been, but British Museum Accounts conclusively establish that the government, not Fellows, paid to take the Xanthian Marbles.

* * *

---

[1] Treasury Register of Papers. Public Offices A–M 1845. British Museum. TNA, T 2/190.

[2] Charles Fellows, *The Times*, 9 May 1842, p. 6; Charles Fellows, *The Xanthian Marbles: their Acquisition, and Transmission to England* (London: John Murray, 1843), p. 6.

[3] Fellows, *The Xanthian Marbles*, p. 40.

[4] G. C. Boase, revised by Elizabeth Baigent, 'Sir Charles Fellows', *ODNB*. Accessed 11 March 2019.

[5] David M. Wilson, *The British Museum: A History* (London: The British Museum Press, 2002), p. 102.

A British Museum display label claims that he had a team at Xanthus.[6] He did not.

The Admiralty recorded: 'Xanthus – Mr. Charles Fellows, the discoverer of these antiquities in Lycia offer his services in their removal, *on condition of receiving a free passage out and home*' [emphasis added].[7] Fellows offered his services to the British Museum: 'I pay my own expenses, but shall expect a free passage out and home ... and rations with the officers'.[8]

Fellows travelled to Xanthus alone. He did not even have an assistant.

* * *

Fellows did not conduct operations at Xanthus.

Between 1839 and 1844, the Admiralty recorded *twenty-nine* entries in the Admiralty Digest under the heading 'Xanthus Marbles' (the Admiralty Digest is explained in Chapter 26). The entries cover: correspondence and directions from the British Museum; correspondence with the Foreign Office; progress reports to the British Museum; directions to HM Ships to transport the marbles; directions relating to stores for the expeditions; and accounts of expenses for the British Museum (including coal for ships) paid by the Treasury. In the twenty-nine entries Fellows is mentioned *once*. 'Xanthus Marbles – Admiral Owen reports on the impracticability of Mr. Fellows' views'.[9]

Admiralty records establish that Fellows did not have any substantive role, but British Museum Accounts state the Xanthian Marbles were acquired under operations 'conducted under the direction of Mr. Fellows'.[10]

However, Fellows pointed out that the arrangements for the expedition were 'made up independently of my accompanying it'.[11] If Fellows was to be in charge, he would not have been excluded from planning the expedition.

* * *

---

[6] 'The Discovery of Ancient Lykia', Nereid Monument (BM Room 17); caption photographed 14 February 2019.

[7] Case 72.6 Freightage of Treasure. TNA, ADM 12/387.

[8] Fellows, *The Xanthian Marbles*, p. 4.

[9] Freightage of Treasure Case 72.2; Case 90a British Museum. TNA, ADM 12/416.

[10] British Museum Accounts 1845 (287). UK PP, p. 9.

[11] Fellows, *The Xanthian Marbles*, p. 5.

Fellows did not excavate at Xanthus, or anywhere else; he was a traveller and adventurer. In 1827, he climbed Mount Blanc by a new route and wrote a book about it.[12] He made drawings (see below), but he did not excavate. Furthermore, there was no need to excavate at Xanthus; the tombs he drew were all monumental and freestanding, one nearly nine metres high.

* * *

Fellows did not bring the Xanthian Marbles to England, as is claimed in the British Museum display label 'Payava's tomb' in Room 20.[13]

The British Museum asked the Admiralty to transport the marbles. The Admiralty recorded: 'Monuments Xanthus: British Museum requests orders be given ... to remove and bring home certain ancient monuments discovered at Xanthus'.[14]

Following the museum's request, HMS *Medea* transported seventy-eight cases of marble from the River Xanthus to Malta in 1842.[15] From there they were transported to England by HMS *Cambridge*; her log book records 'Xanthus Marbles' being discharged at Portsmouth over six consecutive days.[16]

HMS *Warspite* transported five cases (too heavy for *Medea*) from River Xanthus to Malta in April 1843.[17] These were transported to England by HMS *Vesuvius*. Her log book records 'Xanthian Marbles' loaded in Malta in October 1844 and unloaded in Woolwich in November 1844.[18]

The arrangements for packing and moving the Xanthian Marbles to the River Xanthus were undertaken by the crews of HM Ships, not Fellows' alleged 'team', under directions of Commander Warden of HMS *Medea*.[19]

Fellows played *absolutely* no part in bringing the Xanthian Marbles to England. He left Xanthus *six months before* the first cases were transported from the River Xanthus.

---

[12] Charles Fellows, *Narrative of an Ascent to the Summit of Mount Blanc of the 25 July 1827* (London: printed by Thomas Davidson, 1827).

[13] Caption photographed 21 February 2019.

[14] Case 72.6 Freightage of Treasure, 1839. TNA, ADM 12/360.

[15] HMS *Medea* Log Book. TNA, ADM 53/899.

[16] HMS *Cambridge* Log Book. TNA, ADM 53/306.

[17] HMS *Warspite* Log Book. TNA, ADM 54/316.

[18] *Vesuvius'* log book. TNA, ADM 53/1510.

[19] 'Xanthian Expedition', *The Times*, 11 April 1844, p. 7.

* * *

So, if Fellows did not pay the costs, conduct operations or transport the Xanthian Marbles, what did he do? In a word, he *pointed.* Fellows pointed – simple as that. Fellows offered his services to the museum '*to point out* the objects to be removed'[20] On the 12 October 1841, he wrote to Forshall, Principal Librarian of the British Museum, 'At the request of the Trustees of the Museum, I furnish written instructions for the finding the monuments about to be removed from Lycia'.[21] He wrote that the Admiralty's instructions to captains of HM Ships was to put on board 'such objects as should be *pointed out* by Mr. Fellows'.[22]

* * *

Fellows wrote a book on 'the acquisition of the Xanthus marbles *by the British Museum*' [emphasis added].[23] There is no doubting the British Museum took them. Fellows wrote his book to correct 'Imperfect accounts and misrepresentations [that] were appearing in the public prints'.[24]

The misrepresentations Fellows complained about were intended to distance the trustees from any role in taking the Xanthian Marbles. Despite his protestations, the misrepresentations persisted – and continue to this day, not least in British Museum display labels and the online database.

Fellows' role cannot be misconstrued, because he spelled it out clearly:

> I was applied [engaged] by the Museum to furnish forthwith full instructions as to what objects were to be removed and to make maps, plans, and descriptions as to where each fragment was to be sought by the Captain of such of Her Majesty's ships as might be appointed for the service [transporting them to England].[25]

---

[20] Fellows, *The Xanthian Marbles*, p. 4.
[21] Fellows, *The Xanthian Marbles*, p. 4.
[22] Fellows, *The Xanthian Marbles*, p. 4.
[23] Fellows, *The Xanthian Marbles*, n.p.
[24] Fellows, *The Xanthian Marbles*, n.p.
[25] Fellows, *The Xanthian Marbles*, p. 3.

When Fellows discovered Xanthus, he made drawings, twenty-two of which are in his book along with sixty woodcuts.[26] The trustees of the British Museum saw his drawings and on their recommendation 'the Government has given directions for having these monuments of ancient art brought to this country'.[27]

The trustees fancied the Xanthian Marbles and therefore engaged Fellows to return to Xanthus to pinpoint where to find those the trustees wanted.

* * *

While there had been no need to excavate at Xanthus, there was a need to saw marble. Fellows wrote that the object of the trustees' expedition was 'the bringing away ... of the Harpy Tomb'.[28]

As Fellows pointed out, parts of the Harpy Tomb were heavy and needed to be cut:

> I have therefore marked with black paint the lines for the saw, in order that the sculpture should not be injured. This will reduce the weight of the various parts so they may be packed in cases.[29]

However, the sculptures were injured because they were sawed to a standard size to be packed on HM Ships. Fellows wanted 'an accurate measurement of each stone, in order that the officers of the [Royal] Engineers should calculate the weight: the result of which was, that the 82 cases together weigh 80 tons, the three largest stones weighing 2 tons 1 cwt. each'.[30]

Royal Engineers sawed not only the Harpy Tomb but also the Nereid Monument, the Payava Tomb and the Lion Tomb. All the Xanthian monuments were sliced to Fellows' standard size. He wrote: 'I also did this [cut] with the tomb, with the lions resembling the Persepolitan sculpture'.[31]

The *Oxford Dictionary of National Biography* asserts Fellows

---

[26] Charles Fellows, *A Journal written during an excursion in Asia Minor* (London: John Murray, 1839).

[27] Fellows, *A Journal written during an excursion in Asia*, p. v.

[28] Fellows, *The Xanthian Marbles*, pp. 19–20.

[29] Fellows, *The Xanthian Marbles*, p. 34.

[30] Fellows, *The Xanthian Marbles*, p. 42.

[31] Fellows, *The Xanthian Marbles*, p. 34.

'ensured that antiquities were *carefully* removed and transported to a public collection in the British Museum' [emphasis added].[32] Clearly he did not. The monuments were mutilated. The blame lies solely with the trustees of the British Museum.

The sculptures on the Harpy Tomb *were* severely damaged when it was sawed for no other reason than to reduce the weight to be transported. The wing tips of all four female-headed birds at the corners of the Harpy Tomb have clearly been sliced (see British Museum Room 20 and online).

The mutilation of the Xanthian tombs, one of which was constructed as early as 600 BC, was an act of vandalism. It is shocking because the trustees *knew* from Fellows' drawings that entire tombs could not be taken to England. They used Fellows' drawings to dictate what they wanted from Xanthus, with the full knowledge that taking parts of tombs necessitated sawing and destroying important ancient monuments.

The fact that Royal Engineers sliced the Harpy Tomb to Fellows' specifications (as dictated by the trustees) has been covered up by a clever deception. The marble chamber of the Harpy Tomb was raised on a pillar of limestone standing approximately nine metres high. George Scharf Jnr, an artist, drew the tomb on the limestone pillar as it was *after it had been sliced*. This deception is intended to exonerate the trustees of the British Museum who directed Fellows what to take.

* * *

When the Xanthian Marbles were taken in 1843–4 it was not a secret that the entire procurement operation was funded by the government. For example, *The Illustrated London News* spelled this out with engravings of the sliced Harpy Tomb, 'In the British Museum an exhibition … of a collection of marbles made in Asia Minor … *brought to this country at the expense of the Government*' [emphasis added].[33] Furthermore, *The Times* reported the government's role.[34] The British Museum Accounts (in the public domain) show expenditure on taking the Xanthian Marbles for four consecutive years (see Appendix 1).

---

[32] Boase, 'Sir Charles Fellows', *ODNB*. Access 11 March 2019.

[33] 'British Museum: Exhibition of Marbles from Asia Minor', *The Illustrated London News*, 11 February 1843 vol. 2, no. 41, pp. 97–8.

[34] 'Xanthian Expedition', *The Times*, 11 April 1844, p. 7.

Why, then, are the once transparent roles of the trustees of the British Museum and the British government being covered up today? The answer lies in the wording of the permission granted by the Turkish government to take marbles from Xanthus.

At first the Turkish government refused to grant any permission, objecting 'to the extent and the generality of the demand'.[35] Eventually a permission was obtained with the following condition:

> If, therefore, the antiquities … *are lying down here and there, and are of no use* … [the Sultan] shall make no objection to the Captains [of HM Ships] taking them away … Such are the Sultan's commands, in conformity to which you will act [emphasis added].[36]

The Xanthian Marbles, drawn by Fellows, were clearly intact; there were not '*lying down here and there… of no use*'. The removal of the massive Nereid Monument and entire tombs set on nine-metre-high columns was a flagrant violation of the terms of the permission.

The fiction that Fellows funded, excavated and transported the Xanthian Marbles was created by the trustees to cover up their abhorrent act of vandalism in contravention of the terms of the permission granted. The fiction that Fellows *excavated* was essential to cover up the taking of freestanding monuments.

* * *

The important Xanthian Marbles are not mentioned in Tiffany Jenkins' book *Keeping their Marbles*.

This book explains how marbles ended up in the British Museum. It is not a book about restitution. However, it is difficult to see any reason why the eighty tons of Xanthian Marbles should not be loaded on the next freighter bound for Istanbul. The British Museum Act 1963, which prevents the museum from returning anything is, as explained in Chapter 22, an artificial barrier. The argument that it is important that the Xanthian Marbles are seen under the same roof with other

---

[35] Fellows, *The Xanthian Marbles*, p. 3.

[36] Translation of permission dated 29 November 1841 (Fellows, *The Xanthian Marbles*, p. 11).

marbles (in the main also taken by the trustees) will no longer wash. The Xanthian Marbles were not stolen by third parties and received by the museum in good faith. They were stolen by the trustees *themselves*.

Readers who have never had the opportunity to visit the British Museum should google the Nereid Monument. What the trustees of the museum stole is breathtaking.

* * *

In 1843, at a meeting of the trustees when 'His Grace the Archbishop of Canterbury was in the Chair', a resolution was passed thanking Fellows for his help in taking three important tombs from Xanthus.[37]

In 1860, in a cynical attempt to further distance the trustees from an act of vandalism, Fellows received a knighthood 'in acknowledgement in removing to the British Museum the Xanthian Marbles discovered by him in Lycia'.[38]

When the trustees of the British Museum took eighty tons from Xanthus they knowingly destroyed one of the most important archaeological sites in the world. What remains is a UNESCO World Heritage Site.

---

[37] Fellows, *The Xanthian Marbles*, p. 43.
[38] 'Miscellaneous', *Birmingham Daily Post*, 12 November 1860, p. 3.

CHAPTER 16

Sicily, North Africa and Turkey: George Dennis, British Consul

George Dennis was an expert on Etruscan tombs. He explored hundreds of them between 1842 and 1847. In 1848 he published *The Cities and Cemeteries of Etruria*.[1]

In 1863, the Foreign Office appointed him British Consul at Palermo, Sicily, relocated him to Benghazi, North Africa, at the end of that year, and then moved him to Smyrna, Turkey, in 1867. The contention in this book is that Dennis was employed by the Foreign Office on the recommendation of the British Museum *specifically to excavate tombs* on behalf of the museum. The objects Dennis took from tombs are listed in British Museum Accounts:

- the 1864 Accounts state that Dennis, Consul at Palermo, 'excavated ... at the expense of Her Majesty's Government ... the Greek *tombs* at Centuripae, Terra Nuova and Agrigentum' [emphasis added];[2]
- the 1867 Accounts state that Dennis, Consul at Benghazi, 'made excavations on account of the trustees in the ancient *cemeteries* at Teuchira and Ptolemis, two cities of the Cyrenaica Pentapolis' [emphasis added];[3] and
- the 1871 Accounts state that 'Mr. Dennis was sent by the Foreign Office [as Consul at Smyrna], on the recommendation of the trustees of the Museum, to

---

[1] George Dennis, *The Cities and Cemeteries of Etruria*, 2 vols (London: John Murray 1848, revised 1878).

[2] British Museum Accounts, 31 March 1864. UK PP, 1864 (246), p. 16.

[3] British Museum Accounts, 31 March 1867. UK PP, 1867 (249), p.16.

explore the *tumuli* near Sardes [Sardis] … believed to be the burial places of the Lydian kings'.[4]

The government paid for Dennis' excavations and his expenses. British Museum Accounts (1867 and 1868) include expenditure 'For excavations in Asia Minor under the superintendence of Mr. George Dennis, H.B.M.'s [Her Britannic Majesty's] Vice-Consul at Benghazi'.[5] In 1869, the museum and Treasury corresponded regarding 'Dennis Vice-Consul engaged lately in *exploring cemeteries* in Asia Minor. For allowance of expenses of removing his family' [emphasis added].[6]

The Foreign Office record of officials' 'Statement of Services' states that Dennis was employed in 1865–6 in making explorations in Cyrenaica and in 1867 in researches in Asia Minor.[7]

In 1867, George Hamilton at the Treasury wrote to the Foreign Office that the Treasury had received 'an application from the trustees of the British Museum requesting that a sum of £500 may be applied in making excavations in Asia Minor under the directions of Mr. George Dennis, Vice-Consul at Benghazi'.[8] Hamilton confirmed that 'the 2nd Section of the Consular Act 6 Geo IV C.87, Her Majesty through the Secretary of State, may grant leave of absence to a Consul who, in such case shall be entitled to receive full salary'.

Therefore, Consul Dennis was paid a salary by the Foreign Office to rob tombs for the British Museum.

* * *

The objects Consul Dennis took from tombs entered the British Museum collections as donations from the Foreign Secretary, a trustee of the museum. This is another example of where the line between the British government and the trustees of the British Museum is blurred when it comes to taking antiquities.

British Museum Accounts 1864 state:

---

[4] British Museum Accounts, 31 March 1871. UK PP, 1870–71 (272), p. 17.

[5] British Museum Accounts, 31 March 1867. UK PP, 1867 (249), p. 16.

[6] Treasury Register of Papers. Public Offices A–M, 1869. TNA, T 2/286.

[7] *The Foreign Office List* (London: Harrison and Sons, 1898), p. 96.

[8] Letter from George Hamilton to the Foreign Office, 17 September 1867. TNA, T 12/4.

The following presents have been received during the year: *A collection of Greek Vases, Terra-cottas, and other Antiquities discovered in tombs in Sicily and presented to the British Museum by Earl Russell Her Majesty's Secretary of State for Foreign Affairs.* This most interesting collection is the fruit of excavations made by Mr. George Dennis in Sicily, in 1862–63, at the expense of Her Majesty's Government. Most of the objects … were discovered in Greek tombs at … The following are the most remarkable of these vases … [with a page of descriptions].[9]

Today, the British Museum no longer maintains that this collection came from the Foreign Secretary. Greek vases on display in the museum are captioned 'Given by George Dennis'.[10]

Therefore, the following took place:

- the trustees of the British Museum recommended an expert to open tombs;
- the Foreign Office appointed Dennis as Consul near to three prospective sites, for example 'the burial places of the Lydian kings';
- the Treasury paid;
- the Admiralty transported; and
- the Foreign Secretary (a trustee) donated everything from the tombs to the British Museum.

Dennis was a *tombaroli* – a tomb robber. He made no known archaeological records of the tombs he robbed in Sicily, Cyrenaica and present-day Turkey. Dennis' contribution to the museum collections was celebrated in the first history of the museum (see below). This is no longer the case. In fact, Dennis is not even mentioned in *The British Museum: A History* (Wilson). He is clearly a weak link in the museum's façade of propriety.

Dennis' biographical details in the British Museum collections online database states that he was an 'archaeologist, official, collector'. 'Official' is not a euphemism for British Consul.

In 2016, the museum database listed 900 objects from Dennis.[11] By 2019, the total had increased to 1,312.[12]

---

[9] British Museum Accounts, 31 March 1864. UK PP, 1864 (246), p. 16.

[10] BM Room 20; caption photographed 21 February 2019.

[11] <www.britishmuseum.org/research/collections>. Accessed 13 June 2016.

[12] <www.britishmuseum.org/research/collections>. Accessed 2 January 2019.

This is not unusual. Objects from the museum's vast collection are continually being added to the database. In 2016, reportedly about three million of the eight million objects in the collections were on the database. There may be considerably more to come from Consul Dennis.

In 2019, the provenances of the 1,312 objects were stated to be '57 purchased from George Dennis'; '273 donated by George Dennis'; and '850 excavated by George Dennis'.[13]

The provenances give rise to three issues:

- there is no explanation as to how the 850 objects (not donated or purchased) entered the collections;
- the 275 donations are not reliable. This is because British Museum Accounts described, in detail, *all acquisitions* by donation and/or purchase. The accounts describe the objects Dennis donated: one in 1863, one in 1868, three in 1875, and nine in 1889. According to Museum Accounts, Dennis donated a total of fourteen objects – not 273; and
- the figure of 57 purchases is unreliable too. British Museum Accounts do not record a single object being purchased from Dennis.

There is irrefutable evidence (in British Museum Accounts) that the government paid for the excavations of a salaried Foreign Office official. Therefore, what Dennis took from tombs was clearly not his property to either sell or donate.

* * *

In 2016, the British Museum held its blockbuster exhibition *Sicily: Culture and Conquest.*

The *majority* of the objects from Sicily in this exhibition were not from the museum collections. They were on loan from third parties.

Fifty objects were from the museum collections. In display labels, not one of the fifty had either a provenance or museum registration number.[14] Dennis was not mentioned in the exhibition, but a small number of objects were identifiable

---

[13] <www.britishmuseum.org/research/collections>. Accessed 2 January 2019.
[14] A small number had findspots, e.g. found in tomb 7 at Tharros, but no excavator or date.

(from photographs on the British Museum online collection database) as taken by Consul Dennis.[15]

But the real surprise at *Sicily: Culture and Conquest* was that the British Museum did not put on public display the cream of its collection of Greek antiquities taken from Sicily. The museum may have been embarrassed to show its riches from Sicily taken by a grave robber, recommended by the trustees, and employed by the Foreign Office.

The Greek antiquities in the British Museum, taken by Consul Dennis, *eclipse* those selected by the museum from its collection for *Sicily: Culture and Conquest*. The 1,312 objects from Dennis (as listed on the British Museum online database) include the following, not one of which was exhibited at *Sicily: Culture and Conquest*:

- lekythoi (ancient Greek vessels used for storing oil) attributed to the following painters: The Group of Palermo 16 (440 BC–430 BC); The Icarus Painter (470 BC–460 BC); The Painter of Taranto 2602 (470 BC–460 BC); The Phiale Painter (440 BC–430 BC); The Klügman Painter (440 BC); The Zannoni Painter (460 BC–450 BC); The Painter of Palermo 4 (480 BC–460 BC); The Vlasto Painter (470 BC–450 BC): The Reed Painter (420 BC–400 BC); The Achilles Painter (460 BC–430 BC); The Villa Giulia Painter (470 BC–450 BC); The Gela Painter (540 BC–480 BC); The Painter of London E342 (450 BC–430 BC); The Bowdoin Painter (450 BC–440 BC); The Flying-Angel Painter (500 BC–480 BC); The Charmides Painter (480 BC–460 BC); The Pan Painter (480 BC–460 BC); The Providence Painter (480 BC–450 BC); The Brisesis Painter (480 BC–470 BC); and The Theseus Painter (500 BC);
- neck-amphora (ancient storage jar) attributed to The Berlin Painter (490 BC); The Painter of the Yale Lekythos (470 BC–450 BC); The Painter of Würzburg 234 (540 BC–480 BC); and two to The Red-Line Painter (540 BC–480 BC);
- a pelike (ceramic container) attributed to The Clio Painter (450 BC–440 BC); and

---

[15] For example a terracotta statuette of a woman holding fruit (Western Greek 490 BC, Sicily; British Museum number 1875,0818.10).

- column kraters (large vases for watering down wine) attributed to The Duomo Painter (450 BC–440 BC) and to The Boreas Painter (470 BC–480 BC).[16]

* * *

Dennis' contribution to the British Museum is not mentioned in *Keeping their Marbles* (Tiffany Jenkins).

Consul Dennis is not mentioned in *The British Museum: A History*. The museum's database now states that Dennis *sold* and *donated* to the museum because the British Museum will no longer tell the truth as candidly as the first history of the museum did in 1870:

> *The Sicilian Antiquities* [Greek antiquities found in Sicily colonised by Greeks in the 8th century BC]. *Discovered and excavated by George Dennis (Her Majesty's Consul), under direction from the Foreign Office ...*[17]

---

[16] <www.britishmuseum.org/research/collections>. Accessed 13 June 2016.
[17] Edward Edwards, *Lives of The Founders of the British Museum; with notices of its chief augmentors and other benefactors 1570–1870* (London: Trübner and Co., 1870), p. 40.

CHAPTER 17

Crete: Frederick Guarracino, British Consul

Consul Guarracino, the British Consul at Crete, obtained Roman antiquities from the ancient site of Gortyna for the British Museum.

Gortyna was first inhabited at the end of the Neolithic period (3000 BC) and reached its peak during the 1st–5th centuries AD as an ally of Rome.

In 1862 it was reported that Guarracino took the following:

> The sculptures consist in all of eight large fragments, four of which form the head and neck, a portion of the trunk or body, and the fore and hind parts and the other two are portions of the trunk or body, and the fore and hind parts, and the other two are portions of the hind legs of the bull. Another fragment represents a part of the body of a woman ... and ... a small fragment forms the legs of the female ... To these sculptures Mr. Consul Guarracino has added three heads and fragments of *basso-relievo*, besides several coins found by him ... one of the coins bears the effigy of Jupiter and Europa, evidently *illustrative of the same subject as that of the marbles.*[1]

The British Museum confirmed that Guarracino obtained the following:

> A group in white marble, representing Europa crossing the Sea on the Bull, found at Gortyna in Crete, obtained for the British Museum through Mr. Consul Guarracino and brought to England in Her Majesty's Ship, 'Scourge'.[2]

---

[1] 'Antiquities from Crete', *The Gentleman's Magazine*, vol. 212 (Mar. 1862), p. 302.

[2] British Museum Accounts, 31 March 1863. UK PP, 1863 (155), p. 16.

CHAPTER 18

Cyprus: Charles Newton, Ohnefalsch-Richter and Museum Employees

In *The British Museum: A History*, it is claimed that the museum has 'one of the largest collections of Cypriot art in existence'.[1] It is also claimed that the collection is attributable to the Turner Bequest. This claim is a complete myth.

There are *seven* reasons why the British Museum has one of the largest collections of Cypriot art:

- Britain occupied Cyprus. How this came about is explained below;
- a Cypriot law permitted two thirds of all finds at excavations to be sent to the British Museum;
- the British government controlled the excavation permits on Cyprus;
- the British Museum received a royalty share of all third-party excavations on Cyprus (explained below);
- the trustees of the British Museum took antiquities during the forty years leading up to Cyprus' occupation and there was no prospect they would not take more from Cyprus the moment Britain occupied the island;
- the British government, with trustees of the museum in its highest echelons, had deep pockets when it came to funding British Museum excavations; and
- because of the Turner Bequest.

---

[1] David M. Wilson, *The British Museum: A History*, p. 182.

In 1892, Miss Emma T. Turner made a £2,000 bequest 'to be applied at the discretion of the Trustees of the museum for the purpose of excavation'.[2] The trustees spent the entire bequest excavating tombs on Cyprus and exhausted the bequest in three years (see below). The British government funded excavations on Cyprus for twenty years.

In 1897–8, the museum excavated at Maroni and the Tekké (a sacred tomb at Larnaca) 'with the Bequest of the late Miss E. T. Turner'. However, British Museum Accounts show that, by then, only £16 of the bequest remained and so the excavations were 'continued from the Parliamentary Grant'.[3] The government paid in 1898 and for years thereafter.

* * *

The following is how Britain came to occupy Cyprus. In 2019, a large notice at the entrance of Room 72 in the British Museum reads:

> ANCIENT CYPRUS
> The island of Cyprus ... has been inhabited for at least 12,000 years ... Major political powers fought for control over Cyprus because of its strategic location in the Eastern Mediterranean.

Cyprus was coveted. But in 1878, Turkey gave the island to Britain when they formed a defensive alliance whereby Britain agreed that, if Russia attacked Turkish territories in the Ottoman Empire, Britain would defend 'them by force of arms'. In return for this promise, Turkey assigned 'the Island of Cyprus to be occupied and administered by England'.[4]

Cyprus became a British Protectorate. What took place there while under Britain's protection deserves special mention in the history of the formation of the British Museum collections.

A Cypriot law, adopted in 1874 while the island was under Turkish rule, provided that a third of the finds of any permitted

---

[2] British Museum Accounts. 31 March 1893, UK PP, 1892–93 (375), p. 16.
[3] British Museum Accounts. 31 March 1898, UK PP, 1897–98 (174), pp. 9 and 14.
[4] Convention between Great Britain and Turkey, in 'Correspondence respecting the Convention between Great Britain and Turkey of 4 June 1878', Enclosure No. 2. UK PP, 1878, paper no. C2057.

excavations were to be handed to the government of the island and deposited in the Museum of Nicosia.[5] This meant that when Britain occupied the island, the remaining two thirds of everything excavated could go to the British Museum.

The British government granted excavation permits and, in doing so, did little to protect Cyprus' cultural heritage. The government granted preferences to the British Museum and licences to private parties to excavate for their own profit. The power to grant licences to dig for antiquities was not devolved to the Legislative Council, made up of Britons and Cypriots and established on Cyprus, which would have been the appropriate forum. Instead, the power was kept in the hands of the government in London, where the prime minister, the Foreign Secretary and all cabinet ministers were automatically trustees of the British Museum. So no Cypriots, who would have protected their heritage by regulating permitted excavations, were allowed to be involved in granting licences.

Cyprus was one of the few places in the classical world where it was possible to excavate under a government licence.[6] The evidence that the British government granted licences to private parties to excavate for their own profit is in the government's reply to a question in the House of Commons in 1889:

> Digging for antiquities cannot take place in Cyprus except under permit from the Government, which usually reserves to itself a share by way of royalty ... Her Majesty's Government have decided not to issue any further licences (except, perhaps under very special circumstances) to private parties desiring to export the antiquities *for their own profit* or benefit, but only to institutions like the Cyprus Museum, the British Museum, the Berlin Museum etc. [emphasis added].[7]

The royalty share went directly to the British Museum. The above mentioned self-imposed restraint on granting licences to private parties was only adopted by the government *eleven years* after Britain occupied Cyprus.

---

[5] A. S. Murray, et al, Preface, *Excavations in Cyprus* (London: The Trustees of the British Museum, 1900), n.p.

[6] Wilson, *The British Museum*, p. 182.

[7] Baron H. De Worms, HC Deb, 1 Aug. 1889, vol. 339, c54.

In *The British Museum: A History* (Wilson) it is claimed that 'from 1893' a Keeper was able '*to initiate*' excavations in Cyprus through the Turner Bequest.[8] This is factually incorrect. The British Museum initiated excavations in Cyprus fourteen years *before* the Turner Bequest with government funding. British government funding for excavations in Cyprus began in the year Britain occupied Cyprus (see Appendix 1).

The trustees wasted no time in taking antiquities from Cyprus, and began excavating immediately after Britain's occupation in 1878. They continued to do so over the next two decades.

In April 1879, the trustees sent Newton, who by then had been digging for the museum for twenty-seven years, to Cyprus.[9] In August 1879, it was reported that 'Mr. C. T. Newton proposes to commence excavations in Cyprus as soon as possible'.[10]

In Cyprus, Newton met Max Ohnefalsch-Richter, a German archaeologist and dealer, called 'Mr. O. Richter' in British Museum Accounts. When Newton returned to London, Ohnefalsch-Richter was appointed the museum's official archaeologist in Cyprus.[11]

Ohnefalsch-Richter wrote that he was recommended to Newton towards the end of 1879 and that Newton 'entrusted me with the conduct of the first excavations',[12] where he had '100 men working for [him]'.[13] His workmen were paid for by the British government (see below).

British Museum Accounts (for the years 1883, 1884 and 1885) list, as additions to the collections, 'Antiquities discovered by Mr. O. Richter in excavations in Cyprus'.

The British Museum, possibly out of embarrassment, decided to bury everything taken by Ohnefalsch-Richter. The way this was done was by bundling together what he took with objects excavated at subsequent Turner Bequest-funded excavations. This can be illustrated by examining the contents of one tomb – Tomb 93 at Enkomi.

---

[8] Wilson, *The British Museum*, p. 182.

[9] Debbie Challis, *From the Harpy Tomb to the Wonders of Ephesus* (London: Duckworth, 2008), p. 172.

[10] 'Antiquities at Cyprus', *The Times*, 2 August 1879, p. 9.

[11] Challis, *From the Harpy Tomb to the Wonders of Ephesus*, p. 172.

[12] Max Ohnefalsch-Richter, *Kypros: The Bible and Homer* (London: Asher & Co. 1893), p. viii.

[13] Ohnefalsch-Richter, *Kypros*, p. 10.

* * *

Instead of sharing finds one third/two thirds (in accordance with the law of Cyprus), it was decided not to split the contents of any one tomb. Therefore, the British Museum was allocated 267 tombs on Cyprus, of which sixty-two were at Enkomi, a small inland town. These tombs were excavated in 1896 by A. S. Murray of the British Museum with the benefit of the Turner Bequest. Murray (and other museum employees who excavated at other places on Cyprus with the Turner Bequest) wrote an account of his excavations in which he listed the contents of all sixty-two tombs at Enkomi.[14]

In 2019, the British Museum displayed the contents of Tomb 93 at Enkomi '*in their entirety*.'[15] However, the display includes objects that Murray did not find. For example, the centrepiece of the museum's display is an Egyptian broad collar necklace made of strings of gold pendants (153 gold pieces).[16] This is not listed by Murray as found in Tomb 93, or in any other tomb excavated at Enkomi. Murray did find, in Tomb 93, an 'Egyptian pectoral of gold, inlaid with paste, blue pink and white' (119 pieces). This is photographed 'full size' in Murray's book.[17]

The museum's display includes the following from Tomb 93, all of which are in *perfect condition*: a large pottery bell-shaped *krater* (bowl); a pottery stirrup-jar; a pottery tankard; and two terracotta female figurines. However, Murray described Tomb 93 as a cave with a short entrance passage. He drew a diagram to scale. The passage is five feet, the tomb 8ft x 8ft.[18] He wrote: 'This tomb (93) … was found about 8 ft. below the surface; fallen in, and full of rocks and earth with bones interspersed'.[19] Pottery cannot have survived intact. Murray found fragments.

The museum includes two pottery fragments but not the fragment Murray wrote about (and sketched) that 'represents a contest of two athletes'.[20]

---

[14] A. S. Murray, A.H. Smith and H.B. Walters, *Excavations in Cyprus*. Bequest of Miss E. T. Turner to the British Museum. (London: The Trustees of the British Museum, 1900).

[15] BM Room 12; label photographed 14 February 2019.

[16] GR 1897.4-1.535. BM Cat Jewellery 581.

[17] Murray, Smith and Walters, *Excavations in Cyprus*, Plate V.

[18] Murray, Smith and Walters, *Excavations in Cyprus*, p. 5.

[19] Murray, Smith and Walters, *Excavations in Cyprus*, p. 37.

[20] Murray, Smith and Walters, *Excavations in Cyprus*, p. 9.

There are many more objects in the museum's display than Murray described finding in Tomb 93. The following may explain why.

The British Museum excavated at Enkomi with the Turner Bequest in 1896, but that was not the first time the museum had excavated there. The museum had excavated at Enkomi *fifteen* years earlier. British Museum Accounts (1881–2) describe 126 objects 'discovered in excavations … from Enkomi'.[21] The objects listed in the 1881–2 accounts included: gold ornaments; ivory; porcelain; fictile vases; and vases. The objects taken from Enkomi in the British Museum Accounts 1896–7 are grouped under six categories: (1) gold ornaments; (2) ivory reliefs; (3) hermatite; (4) porcelain; (5) fictile objects; and (6) vases.[22]

Therefore, the class of objects taken in 1881 and those taken in 1896 are more or less a perfect match.

* * *

The bundling together of the objects excavated at Enkomi in 1881 with those excavated in 1896 (funded by the Turner Bequest) serves four purposes. Firstly, it means that the British government-funded excavations prior to the Turner Bequest can effectively be buried; secondly, it adds credence to the claim that a Keeper was, through the Turner Bequest, able '*to initiate*' excavations in Cyprus; thirdly, the antiquities that Ohnefalsch-Richter took when he was the museum's superintendent do not have to be mentioned in British Museum Room 72, Ancient Cyprus – and they are not; and fourthly, it is possible to claim that 'one of the largest collections of Cypriot art in existence' is wholly attributable to the Turner Bequest.

The British Museum Cypriot collection is attributable to the seven reasons mentioned above, one being twenty years of sustained government funding – bar the three years funded by the Turner Bequest.

---

[21] UK PP 1881–82, paper no. 231, p. 25.
[22] British Museum Accounts for the year ended 31 March 1897. UK PP, paper no. 326, p. 57.

CHAPTER 19

Chaldea: Hormuzd Rassam, British Vice-Consul

The Chaldean Empire, in present-day Iraq, was pre-Assyrian. On 9 August 2018, *The Guardian* and *The Times* ran near identical headlines:

> British Museum cracks case of looted Iraqi art[1]
>
> British Museum cracks cold case of Sumerian treasures looted from Iraq[2]

The similar headlines, on the same day, indicates that the story was not the result of investigative journalism. It was fed to newspapers worldwide. Researching the story has startling results.

The newspapers reported that, in 2003, the Metropolitan Police seized eight small artefacts from a London dealer which they believed had been looted from Iraq in 2003 after the fall of Saddam Hussein. No progress was made for fifteen years until Scotland Yard's art and antiques squad handed the artefacts to the British Museum for analysis.

Cuneiform inscriptions on the artefacts enabled the museum to pinpoint the exact site from where they were stolen. It was 'Tello [in Chaldea] ... one of the oldest cities on earth, recorded in the earliest form of true written language'.[3]

---

[1] Maeve Kennedy, 'British Museum cracks case of looted Iraqi art', *The Guardian*, 9 August 2018, p. 19.

[2] David Sanderson, 'British Museum cracks cold case of Sumerian treasures looted from Iraq', *The Times*, 10 August 2018, p. 20.

[3] Kennedy, 'British Museum cracks case of looted Iraqi art', p. 19.

This triumphal discovery arose from the 'extraordinary coincidence [that] the [British] museum had an archaeologist, Sebastian Rey, leading a team of archaeologists at the site uncovering the holes in the mud-brick walls of the temple they were taken from, *and the broken pieces the looters had discarded*'.[4]

These are extraordinary, if not incredulous, coincidences. St John Simpson, the senior curator of pre-Islamic collections, is quoted as saying, 'We could trace them not just to the site but *to within inches* of where they were stolen from ... This is a very happy outcome ... nothing like this has happened for a very, very long time, if ever' [emphasis added].[5]

However, if the story had been researched, the following would have been discovered:

- the British Museum has 820 clay cuneiform tablets and artefacts taken *from the same temple* at Tello (spelled Teilo by the British Museum);
- the British Museum provenance for the objects from Tello is 'Acquired from Hormuzd Rassam';[6] and
- the British Museum acquired a staggering 52,747 objects from Hormuzd Rassam.[7]

The museum's online database has no biographical information on Rassam. The following reports, in chronological order with emphasis added, clearly establish that the provenance of *all* 52,747 objects allegedly 'acquired' from Rassam were in fact 'Taken for the British Museum by Hormuzd Rassam under directions of the Trustees':

- '*the trustees of the British Museum* commissioned Mr. Rassam to carry out the [Assyrian] expedition';[8]
- 'Mr. Hormuzd Rassam ... returned from his last archaeological expedition to Assyria, undertaken *under the auspices of the British Museum*';[9]
- 'Mr. Rassam's ... explorations [in Chaldea] *on behalf of the trustees of the British Museum*';[10] and

---

[4] Kennedy, 'British Museum cracks case of looted Iraqi art', p. 19.

[5] Sanderson, 'British Museum cracks cold case of Sumerian treasures looted from Iraq', p. 20.

[6] British Museum database online. Accessed 12 August 2018.

[7] British Museum database online. Accessed 16 August 2018.

[8] 'Assyrian Discoveries' *The Times*, 24 August 1878, p. 4.

[9] 'Assyriology', *The Times*, 4 July 1879, p. 4.

[10] 'Chaldean Explorations', *The Times*, 25 May 1882, p. 4.

- 'explorations carried out by Mr. Hormuzd Rassam *on behalf of the trustees of the British Museum* in Assyria and Babylonia resulted in the addition of some thousands of inscriptions and monuments to the collections'.[11]

In 1864, *The Illustrated London News* published a feature with Rassam's Assyrian discoveries.[12]

Rassam was employed by the British Museum. On 7 August 1878, the Treasury sent a letter to the museum recorded by the Treasury as 'Mesopotamia. For sanction to increase Mr Rassam's personal allowance whilst *employed* in' [emphasis added].[13] A letter dated 24 November 1880 from the British Museum to the Treasury was recorded by the Treasury: 'Assyrian and Babylonian excavations. For sanction to provisions in estimates 1881–2 for and to *re-employment* of Mr. Rassam' [emphasis added].[14]

Rassam wrote, 'I was asked by the British Museum authorities to undertake the superintendence of the excavations in Assyria ... I did not hesitate to accept the proffered honor'.[15] He explained: 'I was the only agent of the trustees who was privileged to export antiquities out of the country [Assyria]'.[16]

Therefore, Rassam was employed by the trustees and consequently everything he took belonged to the museum. It is patent nonsense that the British Museum acquired 52,747 objects from him.

* * *

Rassam published a first-hand account of his discoveries in Assyria with a section titled 'Excavations at the Mound of Tel-Loh [Tello]' where he arrived on 2 March 1879.[17] This is the very temple the British Museum identified as the source of the looted antiquities in the Metropolitan Police's cold case.

---

[11] 'Oriental Inscriptions in the British Museum', *The Times*, 14 October 1884, p. 7.

[12] 'Recent Assyrian Discoveries by Mr. Rassam', *The Illustrated London News*, 16 November 1878, pp. 464–6.

[13] Treasury Register of Papers. Public Offices A–M, 1878. British Museum. TNA, T 2/322.

[14] Treasury Register of Papers. Public Offices A–M, 1880. British Museum. TNA, T 2/330.

[15] Hormuzd Rassam, *Asshur and the Land of Nimroud: being an account of the discoveries made in the ancient ruins of Nineveh, Asshur, Sepharvaim, Calah, Babylon, Borsippa, Cuthah and Van* (New York: Eaton & Mains, 1897), p. 54.

[16] Hormuzd Rassam, Letter to the Editor, *The Times*, 5 April 1894, p. 14.

[17] Rassam, *Asshur and the Land of Nimrud*, p. 276.

Objects, taken by Rassam from Tello, were put on public display at the British Museum in 1884. Antiquities in a new Assyrian Room were

> supplemented by most valuable additions from Mr. Rassam's recent discoveries ... beginning with the monuments of the ancient days of the Chaldean Empire ... Earlier however than this [3750 BC] are *the cones from Tel-Ho* [Tello] and the black granite socket of a gate [emphasis added].[18]

Rassam explained how he found the 4000-year-old cones with cuneiform inscriptions previously unknown to Europeans:

> I placed a number of gangs of workmen to excavate at different parts of the mound ... we came upon the remains of a temple, where I found ... two pebble sockets at the entrance for the posts of the door to revolve upon. One of these I brought home to the British Museum [the granite socket referred to above by the museum] and the other I gave to the Ottoman authorities for the Imperial Museum at Constantinople ... In some parts of the area we had only to dig one foot or two, and came upon inscribed objects, the majority of which consisted of *curiously-inscribed symbols in the shape of a thick, short tent-peg*: but no one has, as yet, found out what these objects represented. There must have been thousands of them in existence at one time, as the whole mound was covered with fragments of them [emphasis added].[19]

The article in *The Guardian* refers to tent-pegs, the term used by Rassam. The looted objects 'included cone-shaped ceramics with cuneiform inscriptions identifying the site as Tello'. There is a photograph of a 'peg-shaped' temple adornment.[20] The article in *The Times* refers to a 'cone', and this too is photographed. A senior curator at the British Museum is quoted as saying that the looted artefacts could be traced '*to within inches*' of where they were stolen from.[21]

---

[18] 'Assyrian Antiquities at the British Museum', *The Times*, 19 January 1884, p. 6.

[19] Rassam, *Asshur and the Land of Nimrud*, p. 276.

[20] Kennedy, 'British Museum cracks case of looted Iraqi art', p. 19.

[21] Sanderson, 'British Museum cracks cold case of Sumerian treasures looted from Iraq', p. 20.

This clearly could also be established by comparing them with those taken by Rassam from the temple at Tello in the museum collections. There was no need to look for 'the holes in the mud-brick walls of the temple they were taken from, and the broken pieces the looters had discarded'.[22] However, the explanation given to newspapers avoids having to disclose that the British Museum sits on *eight hundred and twenty* artefacts taken from the temple at Tello.

* * *

The *eight* looted artefacts identified by the British Museum were presented to the Iraqi ambassador at a ceremony at the British Museum. Hartwig Fischer, the Director of the museum, said they were 'absolutely committed to the fight against illicit trade and damage to cultural heritage'.[23] He added, 'The return of these objects is particularly poignant given the connection to Tello, one of the sites currently being excavated by the Iraq scheme.'[24]

The Iraq scheme is funded by the British government to train Iraqis in retrieval and rescue archaeology. Iraqis should train their sights on the British Museum, in particular on the objects in the over 500 cases that the British Museum took from Assyria (see Chapter 10). The museum will have detailed inventories of the contents of the cases.

The cones with cuneiform inscriptions taken from Tello are the tip of an iceberg. Incriminating evidence has been published of the cuneiform inscriptions taken by the British Museum. Consider the summary of the first of five volumes of *A Selection from the Historical Inscriptions of Chaldaea, Assyria and Babylonia* published by H. C. Rawlinson, who took antiquities from Assyria on directions of the trustees of the museum (see Chapter 10):

> The Inscriptions in this Volume record the names and titles of twenty-five of the early Monarchs of Chaldaea previous to the rise of the Assyrian Empire, of about thirty Assyrian Monarchs between the 13th and the 6th

---

[22] Kennedy, 'British Museum cracks case of looted Iraqi art', p. 19.

[23] Sanderson, 'British Museum cracks cold case of Sumerian treasures looted from Iraq', p. 20.

[24] Sanderson, 'British Museum cracks cold case of Sumerian treasures looted from Iraq', p. 20.

century B.C., and of five Babylonian Kings, who reigned from the fall of Nineveh to the taking of Babylon by Cyrus the Great.

Some hundreds of Kings are also named, who reigned over different portions of Western Asia contemporaneously with these Sovereigns of Ur, Nineveh, and Babylon.[25]

The Historical Inscriptions taken under the directions of the trustees of the British Museum were the archives and tablet libraries of the Chaldeans, Assyrians and Babylonians.[26]

In light of their tenacity with respect to just *eight* objects looted from Iraq, a copy of this book has been sent to Scotland Yard's art and antiques squad and to the Iraqi ambassador who was presented with the eight looted artefacts.

Hormuzd Rassam: postscript

On 27 July 1892, Austen Henry Layard, who took Assyrian antiquities for the British Museum (see Chapter 10), wrote an angry letter to *The Times*:

> Sir, … the notice of the Babylonian and Assyrian collections in the recently published 'Guide to the Exhibition Galleries of the British Museum' … is in several respects inaccurate; but it is against the great injustice done in it to Mr. Rassam that I desire to protest … in the introduction it is stated that this 'unrivalled collection' is due to myself, Sir Henry Rawlinson, and others, and no mention is made of Mr. Rassam … Mr. Rassam was a great 'discoverer' and 'excavator' … but his name has been omitted … During his employment under the trustees of the British Museum, Mr. Rassam discovered the remains of five Babylonian palaces and temples … three temples and one palace in Assyria … I fear that a deliberate attempt is being made to deprive him of the credit which is due. I cannot for one moment believe that … the trustees have countenanced this treatment of Mr. Rassam, who during very many years rendered them the most loyal … services.[27]

[25] H. C. Rawlinson, *A Selection from the Historical Inscriptions of Chaldaea, Assyria and Babylonia*, 5 vols (London: Lithographed by R. E. Bowler, 1861), vol. 1, p. 5.
[26] 'The Literature of the Assyrians and Babylonians', *The Times*, 3 June 1879, p. 11.
[27] A. H. Layard letter to *The Times*, 27 July 1892, p. 8.

The Principal Librarian of the British Museum replied in *The Times* that it was impossible to include everyone in a popular guide-book: 'No disrespect for Mr. Rassam was intended by silently including him under the words "and others".'[28] In a further letter to *The Times* Layard rubbished the museum's reply.

In 1892, Layard feared 'that a deliberate attempt' was being made to deprive Rassam of credit due. Layard was right. At the time of writing, the British Museum online database has objects 'acquired from Hormuzd Rassam' but no biographical information and nothing, therefore, of his achievements or his books in which he explains that he was employed by the museum. The absence of biographical information avoids having to disclose that Rassam was employed by the trustees when he obtained the 52,747 objects which the museum claims were acquired from him.

---

[28] E. Maunde Thompson, 'Mr. Rassam', *The Times*, 29 July 1892, p. 6.

CHAPTER **20**

Mount Aaron: Edward Rogers, British Consul

In 1863, Edward Rogers, the British Consul at Damascus, excavated at one of the holiest sites in Petra, Jordan – Mount Aaron known as Hauran. It is venerated as the resting place of Prophet Haroun by Muslims, by Jews (Prophet Hauran is Aaron, Moses' brother) and by Christians.

In the mid-fourteenth century a small shrine was built on the spot where Aaron is believed to have been buried. Consul Rogers went there and excavated.

In 1865, the British Museum confirmed that Rogers took

> a stone door, sculptured in imitation of bronze, from the Hauran, a colossal bust in high relief, representing a man, or deity, holding a cornucopia, from the temple erected in honour of Herod Agrippa, at Siah, near Kunawat, in the Hauran, three other sculptures from the same district, and two circular covers of marble with Byzantine inscriptions from Palmyra.[1]

The above is not necessarily all that he took. It is what the trustees disclosed that Consul Rogers took. As explained in Chapter 13, Consul Crowe advised the trustees that he found eight sarcophagi in Cyrene. In the British Museum Accounts, the trustees said that he found two.

Consul Rogers' excavations were funded by the British Museum. The evidence is in the museum's 1867–8 accounts:

---

[1] British Museum Accounts for the year ended 31 March 1865. UK PP, 1865 (277), pp. 14–15.

'Amount in the hands of Mr. Consul Rogers for Excavations in the Hauran – £214 4s 4d'.[2]

The Admiralty transported Rogers' finds at the request of the British Museum:

> Antiquities from Jebel Haroun [Mount Aaron] procured by Consul at Damascus. Conveyance to England in a Vessel of War requested by British Museum.[3]

The antiquities were transported to England by HMS *Phoebe*.[4]

* * *

Revered objects from Mount Aaron were taken and buried in storage at the British Museum for no intent, purpose or reason other than that the trustees operated a policy of cultural hoarding (see Chapter 22).

---

[2] British Museum Accounts for the year ended 31 March 1868. UK PP, 1867–68 (254), p. 3.

[3] Admiralty Digest 1863, Case 90a British Museum. TNA, ADM 12/736,

[4] Admiralty Digest 1863, Case 90a British Museum. TNA, ADM 12/736.

CHAPTER 21

Jerusalem: Lieutenant Charles Warren, R.E.

In May 1869, when the Holy Land was part of the Ottoman Empire ruled by the Sultan in Constantinople, the Governor General of Syria and Jerusalem granted Lieutenant Warren (Royal Engineer) a twelve-month permit to carry out archaeological researches and excavation for antiquities in Jerusalem. The permission stated:

> Lieutenant Warren ... should be allowed to make excavations (under certain conditions) at localities where *antiquities* are likely to be found; but he should *on no account* be permitted to make excavations at the Haram Al-Sharif [Temple Mount], the Medjid Omar [Mosque of Omar], the Kubbet es Sakhra [Dome on the Rock] or at any other place in the immediate vicinity of the said Haram Al-Sharif [emphasis added].[1]

Within two months, the British Ambassador in Constantinople had unsuccessfully attempted to have the condition in the permission removed. The ambassador reported to the Foreign Secretary that the Turkish government could not entertain the request that Lieutenant Warren have permission 'to examine the inside of the Haram Area'.[2]

In the following month, another attempt was made to remove the condition but it too failed. The ambassador advised the Foreign Secretary that he had communicated to the Porte (the Turkish government) 'the Foreign Secretary's expression

---

[1] Translation of Firman granted by Gov. Gen. of Syria & Jerusalem to Lieutenant Warren, 1 May 1869. TNA, FO 78/2075.

[2] Letter from Henry Elliot to Earl of Clarendon, 12 July 1869. TNA, FO 78/2076.

of the hope of Her Majesty's Government that the Porte would reconsider its refusal to allow Lieutenant Warren to carry on his excavations at Jerusalem within the Haram Area'.[3]

The ambassador wrote that the Turkish government response to this latest request was that the permission could not be granted

> on account of the well-known fanaticism of the Arabs, whose religious feelings the Sultan could not venture to shock without endangering the public peace.[4]

In the preceding year the Pasha of Jerusalem halted Warren's excavations in Jerusalem (carried on under an earlier permit granted to the Palestinian Exploration Fund) because Warren was excavating at the Mosque of Omar, which was 'contrary to the express terms' of his permission.[5]

The permission granted to Warren in May 1869 was to excavate 'for antiquities' in Jerusalem. If found, they would be destined for the British Museum. Imagine if, by way of inducements and preferences, the Foreign Secretary (a trustee of the British Museum) had succeeded in removing the condition in the permission. Imagine if 'The British Engineer Officer Mr. Charles Warren' (as he is described in the Turkish government permission) was granted licence to inflict on The Temple Mount and other sacred sites in Jerusalem what Royal Engineers, with stone-cutting saws, had inflicted on the Seven Wonders of the Ancient World at Halicarnassus (Chapter 8), at Ephesus (Chapter 11) and at other ancient sites.

The Turkish government and Arab fanaticism saved sacred sites in Jerusalem from fanatics in Bloomsbury.

---

[3] Letter from Henry Elliot to Earl of Clarendon, 18 August 1869. TNA, FO 78/2077.
[4] Letter from Henry Elliot to Earl of Clarendon, 18 August 1869. TNA, FO 78/2077.
[5] Letter from Henry Elliot to Earl of Clarendon, 2 April 1868. TNA, FO 78/2015.

PART III

CHAPTER 22

Cultural Hoarding

'England is to works of art what the grave is to the dead;
her gates do not open again to let them out.' W. Bürger,
1860.[1]

An estimated ninety-nine per cent of the tons of Assyrian and
Babylonian sculptures and Greek and Roman antiquities that
were taken under the directions of the British Museum trustees
have been in storage since the day they arrived in London over
one hundred and fifty years ago.

The number of objects on public display in the museum has
steadily decreased as display space is sacrificed to retail space.

In 2015, the museum displayed roughly 80,000 of its collection
of eight million objects. It candidly stated that this is only one
per cent of the collections.[2] The museum lent on average
3,823 objects (1,982 to UK displays and 1,841 internationally)
in each of the five years up to 2015.[3] This represents less than
0.05% of the collections.

By 2017, the museum displayed about 53,000 objects when
Hartwig Fischer, the new Director of the museum, stated that he
proposed to cut the objects on display down to 49,000, claiming
'Less will be more'.[4] At the time of writing, there are five shops
in the museum selling books, accessories and reproductions.

---

[1] W. Bürger, *Trésors d'art en Angleterre* (Bruxelles and Ostende: Librairie de
Ferdinand Claassen, 1860), p. 1.

[2] *The British Museum, Fact sheet* (PDF, 2015).

[3] *The British Museum, Fact sheet* (PDF, 2015).

[4] 'Less will be more, says new British Museum chief', *The Times* 4 September 2017,
p. 17.

In addition, the museum has nine online stores. Retail is important business for the museum. There is a recently opened pizzeria to add to the Great Court Restaurant and seven cafes, one outdoors. There will be more retail space. This is because there is free entry to the museum and, as at 2017, the museum's funding from central government remained flat during the preceding decade, resulting in a thirty-five per cent cut in real terms.[5]

If 49,000 objects are on public display, that is 0.6% of the collections.

* * *

In 1858, *The Times* reported, 'A vessel has just arrived bearing for the British Museum 500 cases of antiquities from Halicarnassus and Cnidus ... Where is room to be found for all these things?'[6] As far back as 1861, it was blindingly obvious, when tons of antiquities were being taken by the trustees, that they could never be put on public display: 'It is of little use to bring to London the remains of the ancient art of Asia Minor and of Carthage if they are to be buried in sheds and cellars and no one can see them'.[7]

In 1860, a keeper at the museum wrote of the antiquities taken by Nathan Davis from Carthage (Chapter 14) that 'the British Museum has been enriched by some valuable additions to its stores'.[8] *Additions to stores* is a euphemism for hoarding.

In 1886, it was reported that sculptures, locked in a basement at the museum for over thirty years, were 'stowed in what, with grim appropriateness, is called the "Sepulchral Basement"'.[9]

* * *

The extent to which the museum collections are held in storage can be demonstrated by taking two examples. The first are

[5] Charlotte Higgins, 'Director of the British Museum, Hartwig Fischer, reveals plans for an extensive revamp, but won't be drawn on calls to return plundered works', *The Guardian*, 14 April 2018, pp. 6–7.
[6] 'Halicarnassus', *The Times*, 30 November 1858, p. 7.
[7] 'Carthage and Her remains', *The Saturday Review*, vol. 11 (1861), pp. 249–50.
[8] Augustus W. Franks, *On Recent Excavations and Discoveries on the Site of Ancient Carthage* (London: J. B. Nichols and Sons, 1860), p. 7.
[9] 'The Unexhibited Sculptures in the British Museum', *The Graphic*, 11 September 1886, p. 278.

Greek Classical inscriptions; the second are the Greek and Roman sculptures, taken together because they are catalogued together.

In 1874, the collection of Greek inscriptions was catalogued in four volumes, edited by Newton. It consisted of 1,155 Greek inscriptions with the provenances of Athens, Attica, Areos, Argolis, Argos, Arkadia, Boeotia, Branchidae, Corcyra, Crete, Cyprus, Delos, Ephesus, Halicarnassus, Iasos, Ios, Kalymna, Karpathos, Kassos, Knidos, Kos, Kythera, Lakonia, Lesbos, Megara, Melos, Olympia, Priene, Rhodes, Samos, Siphnos, Smyrna, Telos, Tenos, Thasos, Thebes, Thessaly and Thrace.[10]

As discussed in Chapter 11, the museum had a dedicated 'Classical Inscriptions' room (Room 78) in 2012, a small basement room where approximately thirty of the over one thousand Greek inscriptions were on public display. But by May 2018 Room 78 was closed; at the time of writing it is no longer shown on the handout map of the museum. In 2019, half a dozen of the 1,155 Greek inscriptions were displayed in various rooms. This is not even one per cent of the collection.

Classical inscriptions lose much of their meaning when they are sawed from the imposing temples and edifices on which they were intended to be read, surrounded by mountains, sea and sky. When they are stacked in storage for over one hundred and fifty years they mean little other than that they form part of the eight million objects in the British Museum collections.

The trustees did not only take Greek inscriptions. They did not spare *any part* of the pre-classical and classical world. Assyrian panels were sawed at Nineveh, Nimroud, Khorsabad and Kuyunjik. Roman inscriptions were sawed at Cyrene. Seventy-three Phoenician inscriptions were taken from Carthage by Nathan Davis.[11] Wood took four hundred and sixty-two inscriptions from Ephesus. In 2019, three were on public display in Room 70. Forty-one inscriptions were sawed from the Temple of Athena Polias of which two are in Room 70.[12]

---

[10] C. T. Newton, ed. *The Collection of Ancient Greek Inscriptions in the British Museum* (Oxford: The Clarendon Press, 1874), Parts I, II, III & IV.

[11] Franks, *On Recent Excavations and Discoveries on the Site of Ancient Carthage*, p. 9.

[12] See Newton, ed. *The Collection of Ancient Greek Inscriptions in the British Museum*, Part III.

Wherever Greek and Roman inscriptions were to be found there were always marble sculptures and freestanding statues. As an example, Smith and Porcher took thirty-three inscriptions from Cyrene and they also took one hundred and forty-eight Roman sculptures.[13] In 2019, six of the sculptures were on display – the remaining ninety-six per cent are in storage.

In 1904, the Greek and Roman statues in the British Museum were catalogued. The collection had twenty-one statues of Zeus, twelve of Apollo and thirty-two of Dionysus, the Greek god of wine. Add to these the statues of Aphrodite, Ariadne, Artemis and Athena, etc., of Demeter, Eros, Heracles (and identifiable others), and of muses, athletes, uncertain males and uncertain females and the total number of statues in the collections comes to 2,098.[14]

In 2019, the 'Greek and Roman sculpture' room (Room 23) displayed five freestanding statues, two heads and four sculptures. This is a minute fraction of the collection but the room is aesthetically pleasing. Imagine if the museum had a 'Dionysus Room' with nothing but the thirty-two statues of Dionysus in the collections. The room would be dull and absurd – as absurd as hoarding so many statues of Dionysus and, in 2019, not displaying a single one.

There is absolutely no prospect that the 2,098 statues in the museum's Marble Army can ever be put on public display. As with much else at the British Museum, the statues have been hoarded and stored.

* * *

As the British Museum has pointed out, in 2015 only one per cent of the collection is on display. The museum does not disclose where the ninety-nine per cent is stored. It cannot no longer be in a 'sepulchral basement' in Bloomsbury because, if the museum were an iceberg, then ten per cent of the collections would be visible, not the declared one per cent.

At the outbreak of the Second World War, the National Gallery Collection was stored at Manod, a disused slate quarry in Wales with 'air conditioning, temperature controls and smoke

---

[13] Smith and Porcher, *History of the Recent Discoveries at Cyrene*, pp. 98–108.
[14] See A. H. Smith, *A Catalogue of Sculpture in the Department of Greek and Roman Antiquities, British Museum* (London: Longmans, 1904), vol. 3.

detectors'.[15] It would be logical for the museum to use this and similar sites as depositories. The major part of the British Museum collections have been buried in 'stores' since arriving in London.

* * *

In 1963, an artificial barrier was created to ensure that everything hoarded by the trustees would remain in the museum. The barrier was created at the insistence of the trustees. The following explains how it was erected.

The Treasury, as the source of finance for the museum, was responsible for answering parliamentary questions relating to it. In 1963, a Treasury memorandum on the British Museum Bill included 'Major Notes' and 'Minor Notes'. There were fifteen Major Notes, the first being 'Reasons for introducing the Bill' and the eighth, 'The Elgin Marbles' (the section on the Elgin Marbles was removed before the Treasury file was placed in The National Archives).[16]

A separate Treasury memorandum, concerning the British Museum Bill, reveals that the trustees insisted on a barrier that would prevent them from returning *any* objects in the collections: 'The trustees see strong objections of principle to any provision enabling them to transfer objects from their collections, even within a strictly limited field.'[17] The trustees' strong objections led directly to the enactment of Section 3(4) ('Keeping and inspection of collections') and Section 5 ('Disposal of objects') of the British Museum Act 1963. These sections prohibit the trustees from disposing of objects unless the objects are duplicates, or were made after 1850 and are of printed matter and the museum has a copy, or if the objects are unfit to be kept in the collections.

The above provisions in the British Museum Act 1963 are not set in stone. Parliament waived them in 2004 to allow the museum to return human remains.[18] It was done again in 2009

---

[15] James Marriott, 'How Britain's cultural jewels were saved from the Blitz', *The Times*, 2 July 2019, pp. 8–9.

[16] Background papers to British Museum Act 1963 (1962–63). TNA, T 218/548.

[17] Background papers to British Museum Act 1963. TNA, T 218/549.

[18] The Human Tissue Act 2004, section 47.

to permit the museum to return objects looted by Nazis.[19] Parliament can repeal the provisions in their entirety.

When W. Bürger wrote in 1860 that 'England is to works of art what the grave is to the dead; her gates do not open again to let them out' he was not referring to England's art but to the world's.[20]

The buried part of the museum collection may as well be radioactive – it will *never* again see the light of day.

---

[19] The Holocaust (Return of Cultural Objects) Act 2009.

[20] Bürger, *Trésors d'art en Angleterre*, p. 1.

CHAPTER 23

Britain's Best-Kept Secret: Photographs

Photography was invented in the late 1830s and by the late 1850s it was a popular activity. For the first time in history, drawings and sketches made by travellers and explorers were placed side by side with photographs. Within a short period, there was a market for photographs and they were being sold at auctions in London, Paris, Berlin and other European cities. Between 1860 and 1870, there are records of sixty-nine auctions of photographs and photographic equipment.

In *The British Museum: A History* there is a section titled 'Photography – A Missed Opportunity'.[1] With one exception, referred to below, the history of the museum does not mention that photographs were taken at excavations. This chapter establishes that the antiquities taken from Assyria, Branchidae, Carthage, Cnidus, Cyrene, Ephesus, Halicarnassus and Priene were photographed in situ *before* they were removed. With few exceptions, the photographs have never been published.

Royal Engineer photographers

> All Victorian Sapper officers [Royal Engineers] had a grasp of photography. Many went on to become expert.[2]

Before dealing with photography at specific excavation sites, the role of the Royal Engineer photographer must be explained. They are the ones who photographed on behalf of the British Museum at the museum's excavations.

---

[1] Wilson, *The British Museum: A History,* p. 128.
[2] Keith H. Cima, *Reflections from the Bridge* (Whittlebury: Baron, 1994), p. 11.

Royal Engineers traditionally sketched as a way of making topographical records. However, in 1857 the War Department directed that Royal Engineers should be trained as photographers at the South Kensington Museum (renamed the Victoria and Albert Museum). In 1857, the board of the museum recorded that 'two sappers [Royal Engineers] are to be constantly under instructions in Photography to qualify them for practising the Art at Military Stations'.[3]

In 1858, a school of photography was established at the headquarters of the Royal Engineers at Chatham, the School of Military Engineering known as the SME. Army estimates included, for the first time, expenditure 'For Photographic Instruments and Instruction'.[4]

In 1860, the SME staff included 'A Superintendent of Schools and Instructor in Photography ... and six Supernumerary Color-Sergeants of Royal Engineers as Instructors in Photography'.[5] By 1864, the SME had *fourteen* 'Non-Commissioned Officers acting as Assistant Instructors in Photography'.[6]

The reason why all Royal Engineers were trained as photographers was set out in a military order in 1858:

> The orders to Officers commanding companies to which Photographers are attached, are, to send home periodical Photographs of all works in progress, and to photograph and transmit to the War Department drawings of all objects, either valuable in a professional point of view, or interesting as illustrative of History, Ethnology, National History, Antiquities, etc ...
>
> Photographers with complete sets of apparatus have already been sent to the following places: Cawnpore, Bombay, Canton, Greece, Isthmus of Panama. And similar equipments are now being sent to the Cape, Bermuda, the Rocky Mountains.
>
> These will probably be followed by others sent with every company of Royal Engineers going on Foreign or Colonial Service, so that in a few years there will be a network of Photographic Stations spread over the world,

---

[3] Department of Practical Art, and Science and Art Department Minutes 1864. TNA, ED 28/18, p. 50.

[4] Estimates of Effective and Non-effective Army Services. UK PP, 1857–58 (33), p. 107.

[5] Army Estimates for 1860–61. UK PP, paper no. 60, p. 100.

[6] Army Estimates for 1860–61. UK PP, paper no. 60, p. 100.

acting under a systematic instruction and having its
results permanently recorded at the War Department.[7]

Consider the enormity of what was proposed in 1858, to be
achieved within 'a few years'. It was 'a network of photographic
stations spread over the world acting under a systematic
instruction'. This was a precursor to photographing the globe
by aerial photography and then satellites.

The photographs taken by Royal Engineers were of strategic
importance. Photographs of terrain – mountain ranges,
coastlines and headlands – gave British forces the edge.

In 1860, a Royal Engineer gave a lecture in London 'on
photography and its application to military purpose' and
showed photographs taken by Royal Engineers 'on the Asiatic
boundary in Asia Minor, between Russia and Turkey ... the
Isthmus of Panama ... from India, Singapore, China, St.
Petersburg ... and Varna'.[8] In 1860, Royal Engineers were
photographing in Central Africa, the Crimea, Central America
and the Mediterranean.[9]

It was not only Royal Engineers who took photographs.
In 1858, Captain Spratt of HMS *Medina* had a photographic
apparatus onboard ship when he photographed two of the
sarcophagi in Crete (see Chapter 6). It is not known how many
HM Ships were issued with photographic apparatus.

The prospect of a photograph taken by a Royal Engineer
being released to, say, *The Illustrated London News* was as
remote as the first photographs from military satellites being
contemporaneously published in magazines. The photographs
taken by Royal Engineers were kept secret. Furthermore, the
very fact that they were taking photographs was top secret. The
evidence for this is in the *History of the Corps of Royal Engineers*.[10]
Notwithstanding that all Royal Engineers were trained as
photographers and were taking photographs worldwide, the
three volume history of the Royal Engineers does not contain a

---

[7] Fifth Report of the Science and Art Department of the Committee of Council on
Education. UK PP, 1857–58 [2385], pp. 85–6.

[8] 'United Service Institution', *Morning Chronicle,* 9 June 1860, p. 3.

[9] Report from the Select Committee on the South Kensington Museum. UK PP,
1860 (504), para. 1225.

[10] Major-General Whitworth Porter, *The History of the Corps of Royal Engineers*
(London: Longmans, 1889).

single reference to the Royal Engineers' role as photographers. Furthermore, it does not include the words 'photograph', 'photography' or 'photographic apparatus' anywhere. The history was written by a Major-General in the Royal Engineers in 1889. He either self-censored photography, or all references to it were removed by a military censor.

The photographs taken by Royal Engineers pursuant to the above military order have been buried. But there are four facts that cannot be buried:

- the numbers of Royal Engineer instructors in photography at the School of Military Engineering;
- all Royal Engineers were trained as photographers, which involved learning how to develop films using chemicals;
- the evidence of expenditure on photography by the Army. For example, in the first quarter of 1862 the Army spent more on its 'Chemical and Photographic Establishment (£1,874)' than it did on the 'Department of Inspector of Artillery (£1,369)';[11] and
- Royal Engineers were, from 1858 onwards, under specific orders to take photographs. The orders included photographing 'antiquities'.

That is why Royal Engineers were sent to photograph at British Museum excavations. But they did not at the earliest in Assyria.

Photographing excavations in Assyria

Excavations conducted under the directions of the trustees of the British Museum in Assyria were photographed.

Layard's expedition to Assyria in 1845 (see Chapter 10) has been described as 'the first practical trial for a British-sponsored liaison between photography and archaeology'.[12] The trustees offered Layard a photographic apparatus but he declined, apparently not trusting the early chemical processes.

The trustees sent three artists to Assyria. The last two, Mr Bell and Mr Holder, were sent with a photographic apparatus – a

---

[11] Army Estimates 1862–1863. UK PP, 1862 (50), p. 137.
[12] Mirjam Brusius, 'Photography's Fits and Starts: The Search for Antiquity and its Image in Victorian Britain', *History of Photography*, vol. 40 (London: Routledge, 2016), pp. 250–66.

Talbotype (also called Calotype). This was invented by Henry Fox Talbot who had close collaborations with the British Museum and took one of the earliest photographs of the museum and of objects in the collections.[13]

The trustees subsequently sent William Boutcher to Assyria. He was a draughtsman and a 'photographist'. The trustees instructed him 'to make drawings or photographs'.[14]

There is concrete evidence that photographs were taken in Assyria. Some of the engravings in *The London Illustrated News* were made from photographs (see Appendix 3).

In 1855, it was reported that 'M. Place took photographs of Assyrian marbles'.[15] This photographer does not appear to have had any connection with the British Museum.

Not one single photograph taken in Assyria by Bell, Holder or Boutcher has ever been published by the trustees of the British Museum.

While there are no published photographs of British Museum excavations in Assyria, there are photographs of Jerusalem taken in 1835, over a decade before Layard excavated in Assyria. Seventy-four photographs of Jerusalem were taken by a Royal Engineer (Sergeant McDonald).[16]

The reason why there are published photographs of Jerusalem but not Assyria is because photographs taken in Jerusalem formed part of an ordnance survey and nothing was taken from there. Therefore, the photographs are not incriminating. However, at Nimroud, Nineveh, Khorsabad and Kuyunjik *everything* that could be taken and hacked from the walls of palaces was photographed and then removed under the direction of the trustees of the British Museum who used the photographs to dictate what to take. The excavations in Assyria continued for over three decades (as evidenced by expenditure in British Museum Accounts; see Appendix 1). Photographs were clearly taken, but because they are incriminating they have never been published.

---

[13] Brusius, 'Photography's Fits and Starts', pp. 260–1.

[14] Brusius, 'Photography's Fits and Starts', p. 178.

[15] 'Naval and Military', *Illustrated Berwick Journal*, 8 September 1855, p. 1.

[16] Kathleen Stewart Howe, *Revealing the Holy Land: The Photographic Exploration of Palestine*. Reviewed by Peter Clark in *British Journal of Middle Eastern Studies*, vol. 25, no. 2 (1998), pp. 303–304.

Photographing excavations at Halicarnassus, Cnidus and Branchidae

Newton's *Travels and Discoveries in the Levant* (1865) includes eight engravings captioned 'From a photograph by D. E. Colnaghi'. Colnaghi, with his photographic apparatus, accompanied Newton on his travels. Therefore, Newton was well aware of the benefits of photography before going to Halicarnassus to excavate the mausoleum.

In *The British Museum: A History*, it is claimed that Newton became, by accident, the first person to use photography on a British Museum excavation.[17] In fact, photography was used on British Museum excavations in Assyria a decade before Newton. Furthermore, there was nothing accidental about the photographs taken at Newton's excavations.

When Newton was sent to excavate the Mausoleum at Halicarnassus, he requested that 'one of the Sappers [Royal Engineers] should be a photographer'.[18] The Foreign Office accordingly instructed the War Office that one of four Royal Engineers on Newton's expedition should 'be able to use the Photographic apparatus'.[19] The War Office sent Corporal B. Spackman R.E. and subsequently replaced him with Corporal McCartney R.E., both expert photographers.[20]

The Admiralty recorded, 'Photographic Apparatus. FO [Foreign Office] requests that it may be conveyed to Mr. Newton [at Halicarnassus]'.[21] While in Halicarnassus, Spackman and McCartney were supplied chemicals by Horne and Thornthwaite, London.[22]

Newton wrote that 'upwards of one hundred photographs were taken by Corporal Spackman between November 1857 and January 1858 at Bodrum, Lagina, Geronta and Kos'.[23]

[17] Wilson, *The British Museum: A History*, p. 128.
[18] C. T. Newton, *Travels & Discoveries in the Levant* (London: Day & Sons, 1865), vol. 2, p. 67.
[19] Letter from the Earl of Clarendon to the War Department, 22 September 1856. TNA, FO 78/1334, p. 49.
[20] Letter from C. T. Newton to the Earl of Clarendon, 28 August 1857. TNA, FO 781/1335, pp. 141–2.
[21] Admiralty Digest, 1856, Case 90a British Museum. TNA, ADM 12/624.
[22] Letter from C. T. Newton to the Earl of Clarendon, 20 December 1856. TNA, FO 78/1334, p. 158.
[23] Letter from C. T. Newton to the Earl of Malmesbury, 4 May 1858. TNA, FO 78/1343, pp. 159–62.

Thereafter, many more photographs were taken at Bodrum, Cnidus and Branchidae.

From Bodrum, Newton sent to three successive Foreign Secretaries, all trustees of the museum, letters and progress reports.[24] Parliament was being petitioned to pay for Newton's ongoing excavations, so in order to induce grants for the excavations, Newton's letters to the Foreign Secretaries were presented to parliament in 1858 and 1859.[25]

In his letters and reports, Newton uses the word 'photograph' thirty times, 'photographic' seventeen times, and 'negatives' nine times. Newton's submissions are a valuable resource because they record that he sent the following photographs to the Foreign Office.

From Halicarnassus:
- twelve of the Mausoleum of Halicarnassus;
- a colossal female head;
- three pieces of a frieze;
- an Ionic column;
- foundations;
- a Roman tessellated pavement, 'more than 90 square feet, extending in one direction 115 feet';
- mosaic floors ('Before attempting to take away the floor I had nearly the whole copied by photography');[26]
- a colossal statue; and
- a female hand.

None of these photographs have been published.

From Cnidus:
- photographs of the walls surrounding Cnidus (described in 1863 as 'still almost perfect, as will be seen by Mr. Newton's plates');[27] and

---

[24] Earl of Clarendon (1857–58), Earl of Malmesbury (1858–59) and Lord John Russell (1859).

[25] *Papers respecting the Excavations at Budrum: Presented to both Houses of Parliament by Command of Her Majesty* (London: Harrison and Sons, 1858). UK PP, 1857–8 [2359] [2378]; and *Further Papers respecting the Excavations at Budrum and Cnidus: Presented to the House of Lords by Command of Her Majesty* (London: Harrison and Sons, 1859). UK PP, Series 2 [2575].

[26] Newton, *Travels & Discoveries in the Levant*, vol. 2, p. 81.

[27] 'Halicarnassus, Cnidus, and Branchidae', *The Times*, 4 September 1863, p. 9.

- a set of nine photographs of the colossal Lion from Cnidus (spelled Knidos) being hoisted. One of the nine photographs is incorporated in the display caption in the Great Court at the British Museum with the Lion. Newton is not mentioned, but he is the man standing to the right of the Lion.

From Branchidae:

- another set of nine photographs of the ten statues of seated women that lined the Sacred Way of the Temple of Apollo Didymeus (see Chapter 8).

These photographs have never been published.

* * *

Newton sent photographs to the Foreign Office in small batches, as and when they were taken and developed, but on 6 July 1859 he sent a remarkable document:

> Invoice of Photographic Negatives shipped on board Her Majesty's ship 'Supply,' June 8, 1859 (Cases F, G).[28]

This invoice lists 113 negatives, each with a description of the subject matter of the photograph.

In a separate invoice Newton listed fourteen negatives on waxed paper, ten proofs, fifty-one photographic positives, and one hundred impressions from negatives.[29]

None of the photographs from Bodrum and the other sites excavated have been published with the exception of the Lion of Cnidus being hoisted. There are published photographs of Newton with Lieutenant Smith at an excavation and Newton sitting on a wheelbarrow, but these photographs reveal nothing of what was taken or destroyed.

Newton's invoices, as standalone documents, are an extraordinary and invaluable resource. Furthermore, the

---

[28] *Further Papers respecting the Excavations at Budrum and Cnidus: Presented to the House of Lords by Command of Her Majesty.* 1859. UK PP, Series 2 [2575]), Enclosure 3 in No. 17, p. 102.

[29] *Further Papers respecting the Excavations at Budrum and Cnidus: Presented to the House of Lords by Command of Her Majesty.* 1859. UK PP, Series 2 [2575]), Enclosure 4 in No. 17, p. 102 and p. 103.

invoices are in the public domain because they form part of the papers presented to parliament in 1859.[30]

R. P. Pullan made drawings of the Mausoleum at Halicarnassus. He was under contract to the British Museum, receiving £250 and agreeing to give up all his drawings.[31] Pullan returned to England in 1859 and Newton asked the Foreign Office to send out another draughtsman. The request was refused on the grounds of expense and the assertion that a photographer would be more useful: 'I should have thought that the photographer would be able to do all that you want in regard to architectural drawings'.[32]

The reply establishes that as early as the 1850s, excavating antiquities and photography had become inseparable.

Photographing excavations at Cyrene
Lieutenant Smith, a Royal Engineer-trained photographer, excavated at Cyrene (see Chapter 13). Prior to his departure, Smith wrote to the War Office:

> A photographic apparatus would of course be of the greatest service in taking views of the architecture, sculpture, scenery etc.[33]

Smith's photographs from Cyrene formed an integral part of the reports that Newton prepared for the trustees. Newton's report, dated 22 May 1861, described five sculptures, the following being three:

- 'a colossal statue, about eight feet high ... Apollo ... broken in three pieces ... the head and feet of this statue are represented in *photographs no. 1, 2,* enclosed in Lieut. Smith's No. 3 of March 21 [1861]'. (This statue is in the British Museum, 'Marble statue of Apollo holding a kithera' (Room 22, GR. 1861-7-251), where the caption reads 'it was found broken into many pieces');

---

[30] *Further Papers respecting the Excavations at Budrum and Cnidus: Presented to the House of Lords by Command of Her Majesty.* 1859. UK PP, Series 2 [2575], Enclosure 3 in No. 17, p. 102 and p. 103.

[31] Letter from R. P. Pullan to A. Panizzi, 30 July 1857. TNA, FO 78/1335, p. 67.

[32] Letter from E. Hammond to C. T. Newton, 17 January 1859. TNA, FO 78/1490, p. 197.

[33] Letter from R. M. Smith to General Sir J Burgoyne, 18 May 1860. Admiralty correspondence 1860. TNA, ADM 1/5745.

- 'A group, representing the Nymph Cyrene struggling with a lion ... *photograph no. 3* enclosed in Lieut. Smith's No. 3 of March 21 [1861]' (not on public display in 2019); and
- 'A bearded head ... the portrait of a Roman Emperor ... *photograph no. 6* of Lieut. Smith's No. 4 of April 8' (in 2019 on display Room 70).[34]

One hundred and forty-eight sculptures were taken from Cyrene. They all would have been photographed *in situ*, as would the thirty-three inscriptions taken. Smith's photographs from Cyrene have never been published.

There are sixteen photographs in Smith and Porcher's co-authored book but they were *not* taken in Cyrene. The sculptures are photographed on pedestals in the museum.[35]

* * *

Smith and Porcher made a list of *everything* they took on their expedition to Cyrene:

> Two double circular tents ... two small portable wooden trestle bedsteads ... two field-hospital cork mattresses, two pillows, four blankets, and two rugs ... two iron folding chairs ... cooking apparatus ... A large supply of candles and Lucifer matches; a few simple medicines, some lint, sticking plaster, an axe, two small hatchets, two saws, six spades and pickaxes, a crowbar ... a hammer, and some nails.[36]

They listed plasters and nails – but not the chemicals and the photographic apparatus which Smith specifically requested. However, the photographic apparatus on a tripod is the centrepiece in a drawing made by Porcher of their living quarters in Cyrene, Smith seated on the left with a Union Jack in the foreground (see Plate 1).

It is a surprising mistake that Smith and Porcher included this drawing with the photographic apparatus in their book because they kept out of it the fact that they photographed the antiquities taken from Cyrene.

---

[34] Copy of Report from C. T. Newton Esq., Keeper of the Department of Greek and Roman Antiquities, British Museum, 22 May 1861. TNA, ADM 1/5777.

[35] Smith and Porcher, *History of the Recent Discoveries at Cyrene*, Plates 61–76.

[36] Smith and Porcher, *History of the Recent Discoveries at Cyrene*, pp. 8–9.

Plate 1: Interior of Smith's and Porcher's residence in Cyrene showing camera on tripod. From Smith and Porcher, *History of the Recent Discoveries at Cyrene*, Plate 9.

Photographing excavations at Carthage

Nathan Davis excavated at Carthage (see Chapter 14). In 1857, he wrote to the Foreign Secretary from Carthage:

> I am now awaiting certain chemicals from Europe ...
> I hope to furnish Your Lordship with photographic sketches of Carthage, *as well as of the chief objects hitherto found* [emphasis added].[37]

Davis sent the Foreign Office regular despatches, some with enclosures, which were forwarded to the trustees. Davis' enclosures have not been traced but are presumed to be photographs. This is because Davis' excavations at Carthage were concurrent with Smith's and Porcher's along the north coast of Africa at Cyrene. On three occasions the Foreign Office sent the trustees (under same cover) Davis' despatches (from Carthage) and Smith's (from Cyrene).[38] It is known that Smith's enclosures were photographs because they were incorporated in the progress reports written by Newton for the trustees.

Davis' photographs taken at Carthage have never been published. Furthermore, their very existence has never been admitted.

Photographing excavations at Ephesus

Wood's excavations for the British Museum at Ephesus commenced in 1863 (see Chapter 11). He was assisted by three Royal Engineers, one of whom, Corporal Trotman, took photographs.[39]

In 1865, magic lantern slides of the 'Ruins at Ephesus' were being circulated as education aids at all military schools in England.[40] These slides of Ephesus can only have been taken by the Royal Engineer assisting Wood.

Wood includes a small number of photographs in his book *Discoveries at Ephesus, including the site and remains of the Great*

[37] Letter from N. Davis to the Earl of Clarendon, 13 January 1857. TNA, FO 335/108.
[38] Despatches from Davis and Smith. TNA, FO 78/1335, pp. 224–5; FO 78/1343, p. 38; FO 78/1490, p. 274.
[39] J. T. Wood, *Discoveries at Ephesus, including the site and remains of the Great Temple of Diana* (London: Longmans, Green, and Co., 1877), pp. 194 and 283.
[40] 'Council of Military Education: Second Report on Army Schools, Libraries and Recreation Rooms'. UK PP, 1865, paper no. 3422, p. 196.

Temple of Diana, but given that he excavated at Ephesus for eleven years, the site must have been extensively photographed.

With few exceptions the photographs taken of one of the Seven Wonders of the Ancient World as it was *before* Wood removed sixty tons of marble, as he admitted doing, have never been published.

Photographing excavations at Priene

Photographs were taken at Priene. This was confirmed by E. L. Hicks, who visited Priene and described the Temple of Athena Polias *before* one hundred and ten cases of marble were taken:

> All this, and more, was still there, as Mr. Pullan's photographs and plans testify to those who had not the good fortune to see the ruin in 1870.[41]

Eighty tons of marble was taken from the Temple of Athena Polias at Priene but only after it was photographed by R. P. Pullan. Only thirty-three of Pullan's photographs are known to exist.[42]

Photography at the Chinese emperor's Summer Palace

The destruction of the Summer Palace in 1860 is included in this book, which is concerned with antiquities, for three reasons: Royal Engineers took photographs there; the photographs were suppressed; and, as established in *China's Summer Palace*, a trustee of the British Museum was personally responsible for the destruction of the Summer Palace.[43]

In 1860 there were ten photographers with the joint British and French force in China. Britain had three Royal Engineers (Lieutenant John Ashton Papillion, Corporal John Wotherspoon and Sapper Charles Parker);[44] Felice Beato (attached to British forces); and three accomplished amateurs.[45] The French had

---

[41] E. L. Hicks, 'Judith and Holofernes', *The Journal of Hellenic Studies*, vol. 6 (1885), pp. 261–94; p. 267.

[42] Joseph Coleman Carter, *The Sculpture of the Sanctuary of Athena Polias* (London; The Society of Antiquaries of London with British Museum Publications, 1983), p. 11.

[43] O. M. Lewis, *China's Summer Palace: Finding the Missing Imperial Treasures* (London: High Tile Books 2017), pp. 335–404.

[44] Terry Bennett, *History of Photography in China 1842–1860* (London: Quaritch, 2009), p. 103.

[45] Major M. Dowbiggin, Dr J. Forbes and R. Morrison.

two military photographers (Lieutenant Colonel Charles du Pin and Paul-Emile Berranger) and an official press photographer (Antoine Fauchery, the correspondent of *Le Moniteur*).

Photographs taken in China by the ten photographers in September and November 1860 have been published. However, there are no published photographs of the Summer Palace taken either before or after it was destroyed in October 1860. Beato captioned photographs 'The Summer Palace, Yuen Ming Yuen' and 'The Great Imperial Palace, Yuen Ming Yuen', but these are deceptions. Those photographs of wooden structures were taken at Wanshoushan (Hill of Imperial Longevity), not at the Summer Palace.[46] There are no photographs of the fourteen marble palaces at the Summer Palace.

Photographs taken in October 1860 were censored for two reasons. The first is that photographs would reveal the imperial treasures divided between Britain and France in accordance with the *Convention between Her Majesty and the Emperor of the French, Relative to Joint Captures in China*.[47] The French spoils from China were presented to Napoleon III and exhibited at the Louvre in 1861. The exhibition was covered by *The Illustrated London News*.[48]

Britain's share of China's treasures was in the hands of the 8th Lord Elgin (his father, the 7th Lord Elgin, took the marble sculptures from the Parthenon known as the Elgin Marbles). Elgin was at the Summer Palace acting as Britain's treaty negotiator in China. He was a trustee of the British Museum.

However, most of Britain's share vanished (see below). *China's Summer Palace* identifies over one thousand objects with the provenance 'from the Summer Palace'. Objects were sold by British officers at auctions. Objects are in the Royal Collection, the Victoria and Albert Museum, the British Museum and other collections.[49] However, these objects represent an infinitesimal fraction of the estimated one million objects taken from the Summer Palace.

---

[46] David Harris, *Of Battle and Beauty: Felice Beato's Photographs of China* (Santa Barbara: Santa Barbara Museum of Art, 1999), p. 150.

[47] Original in Miscellaneous prize correspondence. TNA, HCA 30/1006.

[48] 'French Spoils From China', *The Illustrated London News*, 13 April 1861, p. 339.

[49] Lewis, *China's Summer Palace*, pp. 335–404.

The second reason why the photographs taken at the Summer Palace were censored is because they are a record of what was destroyed. The Summer Palace consisted of 'upwards of 200 buildings and the grounds covered an area of eight by ten miles'.[50]

Immediately after China's treasures were divided, Elgin ordered the destruction of the Summer Palace. Elgin claimed he destroyed the Summer Palace as retribution for the Chinese having murdered British prisoners, but the prisoners were alive when the Summer Palace was destroyed. It was actually the other way round – the Chinese killed the prisoners as retribution for the destruction of the Summer Palace. A British officer wrote to his mother from China:

> we burnt the Emperor's palace at Yuan-Ming-Yuan to the ground. It will give you an idea of the extent of the conflagrations when I tell you that 3,500 men were employed for two days burning. Hundreds of buildings were reduced to ashes.[51]

In the House of Lords, the destruction of the Summer Palace was described as 'an act of vandalism which … must justly be ranked with such deeds as the burning of the library of Alexandria or the sacking of Rome by the Constable de Bourbon'.[52]

The Summer Palace was destroyed on Elgin's orders. General Montauban, the French commander in China, flatly refused an offer from General Grant, commander of British forces, to join in the destruction.[53] In the House of Commons, Palmerston, the prime minister, was asked whether the commander of the French forces in China had acquiesced or not in the destruction of the Summer Palace. Palmerston answered, 'I have no hesitation in saying that General Montauban did not acquiesce in the destruction of the Emperor's Palace'.[54] The member who asked was shaken by Palmerston's admission and said he

---

[50] Henry Brougham Loch (Lord Loch), *Personal Narrative of Occurrences During Lord Elgin's Second Embassy to China in 1860* (London: John Murray, 1900), p. 168.

[51] George Allgood, *China War 1860 Letters and Journal* (London: Longmans & Co., 1901), p. 58.

[52] Marquess of Bath, *Hansard*, vol. CLXI (1861) (392).

[53] Letter from General Montauban to Sir Hope Grant, 17 October 1860. China: correspondence from the Earl of Elgin. TNA, FO 17/331, p. 324.

[54] Mr Scully, *Hansard*, HC Deb, 14 February 1861, vol. 161, cc 400–18.

'could hardly have believed that this act was committed on the authority of the English Ambassador [Elgin]'.[55]

China's Summer Palace explains how the treasures were divided by three named British and three French officers. Britain's share should have been put in the hands of Prize Agents and sold in accordance with Prize Law.[56] However, Elgin knew that, having been sent to China to ratify the Treaty of Tientsin, parliament would have been outraged that he had destroyed the Summer Palace. He also knew that parliament would not, in any event, have voted sufficient funds to enable the British Museum to acquire a significant part of China's treasures on the open market (Prize Agents earned 1.5% commission).

Therefore, Elgin destroyed the Summer Palace to cover up that Britain took a half share of the treasures at the Summer Palace. He did this to enrich the British Museum collections.

It is shocking that a trustee of the British Museum personally ordered the destruction of the Summer Palace. It is equally shocking that the trustees destroyed numerous ancient sites during the two decades before Elgin destroyed the Summer Palace in 1860 and in the decades that followed. They also did this to enrich the museum collections.

Photography in Abyssinia

The military campaign in Abyssinia is one of the rare instances where it is admitted that Royal Engineers took photographs and some of their photographs have been allowed to be in the public domain. However, the photographs are those of the terrain and of groups of soldiers, not those of the treasures taken (see below).

In 1868, a British force was sent to Abyssinia (present-day Ethiopia). It included eight photographers from the 10th Company Royal Engineers.[57] The National Archives holds an album of photographs, *Abyssinian Expedition: Photographs 1868–1869*. The album has seventy-eight photographs taken by Royal Engineers.[58] In 1959, Sotheby's auctioned an album

---

[55] Mr Scully, *Hansard*, HC Deb, 14 February 1861, vol. 161, cc 400–18.

[56] Lewis, *China's Summer Palace*, pp. 43–5.

[57] HCPP 1867–68 [3955], p. 313.

[58] Ethiopia 1: Album of sketches and photographs taken by the 10th company, Royal Engineers. TNA, CO 1069/5.

containing sixty-eight photographs taken by Royal Engineers in Abyssinia.[59]

Photography in Abyssinia is included here because the trustees of the British Museum not only targeted antiquities, they coveted Abyssinia's treasures and sent a museum employee with the British force to take treasures.

The trustees asked the government if someone from the museum could accompany the British forces 'to collect inscriptions, coins, gems, manuscripts, ethnological and other objects *as the occasion might offer*, transport them to England, for the trustees of the British Museum' [emphasis added].[60] The trustees pointed out that Abyssinia had one of the oldest Christian Churches in the East and 'it may be reasonably anticipated that numerous ancient manuscripts must have been preserved there'.[61]

The government made a specific grant to the museum: 'Abyssinian Expedition. For a grant of £600 for antiquarian'.[62]

The antiquarian was Richard Rivington Holmes, an employee of the museum. It was reported in parliament that he went to Abyssinia 'for the purpose of collecting any article of worth to add to the collection in the British Museum'.[63]

Mr Spencer Walpole (a trustee of the museum) said in parliament:

> Mr. Holmes, as an officer of the British Museum, accompanied the Abyssinian Expedition, and ... secured articles which Mr. Holmes thought it would be for the advantage of the public that the British Museum should possess.[64]

The trustees were right about the manuscripts. Holmes wrote: '400 books were brought back to England and deposited in the

---

[59] Sotheby's, 27 May 1959, Lot 872.

[60] Letter from J. Winter Jones to the Secretary of State for India, 15 October 1867. UK PP, papers connected with the Abyssinian expedition 1867–68 [3955], p. 370.

[61] Letter from J. Winter Jones to the Secretary of State for India, 15 October 1867. UK PP, papers connected with the Abyssinian expedition 1867–68 [3955], p. 370.

[62] Registers of Papers. Alphabetical A–M, 1867, British Museum. TNA, T 2/278.

[63] Colonel North, *Hansard*, HC Deb, 30 June 1871, vol. 207, cc 939–52.

[64] Abyssinian War – Prize – The Abana's Crown and Chalice. *Hansard*, HC Deb, 30 June 1871, vol. 207, cc 939–52.

British Museum'.[65] They were catalogued by William Wright in the *List of the Magdala Collection of Ethiopic Manuscripts in the British Museum*.[66]

The Royal Collection received loot from Abyssinia. The Gold Crown of the Sovereign of Abyssinia and a Gold Chalice are illustrated in *Naval and Military Trophies & Personal Relics of British Heroes* (1896).[67] The two Abyssinian crowns are listed in the *Classified List of Photographs of Works of Decorative Art in the Victoria and Albert Museum, and other Collections*.[68]

Prior to 1872, Queen Victoria lent ninety-one objects of 'Abyssinian spoils' to the South Kensington Museum (the V&A).[69] The Victoria and Albert Museum obtained loot from Abyssinia, which is listed in *China's Summer Palace*.[70]

Where are the photographs of antiquities taken by Royal Engineers?

The Royal Engineers Museum online catalogue has a small collection of photographs. They include photographs of sappers, groups of sappers, bridges, bridge building and bridge-opening ceremonies. However, there is not a single photograph taken at any of the above excavations where it is known that Royal Engineers photographed. Further, there is not a single photograph of antiquities when it is known that, from 1858, Royal Engineers were under standing orders specifically to photograph antiquities.

The reason why The Royal Engineers Museum does not have photographs of excavations is because the Royal Engineers did not retain them.

Photographs of excavations were sent to the Foreign Office. The Foreign Office forwarded the photographs and despatches

[65] Richard Rivington Holmes, *Naval and Military Trophies & Personal Relics of British Heroes* (London: John C. Nimmo, 1896), n.p.

[66] William Wright, *List of the Magdala Collection of Ethiopic Manuscripts in the British Museum* (Leipzig: Deutsche Morgenländische Gessellschaft, 1875).

[67] More than one gold crown was taken at Magdala. The Crown and Chalice of the Abana was the property of the Treasury. (*List of Objects in the Art Division South Kensington Museum, Lent during the Year 1872* (London: George E. Eyre and William Spottiswood, 1873), p. 44).

[68] *Classified List of Photographs of Works of Decorative Art in the Victoria and Albert Museum, and other Collections* (1901), Part IV, p. 30.

[69] *List of Objects in the Art Division South Kensington Museum, Lent during the Year 1872*, p. 77.

[70] Lewis, *China's Summer Palace*, pp. 249–50.

to the British Museum with instructions to make copies of the despatches and return the originals *together with the photographs.*[71]

It is not known where the Foreign Office stored negatives and photographs in the mid to late 1800s, and it is not known where they are held today.

If the temperature and humidity in a disused Welsh slate quarry permitted storing the National Gallery Collection during the Second World War, then photographs and negatives can be archived there today. However, there is a recently discovered secret Foreign Office depository.

In April 2011, the Foreign Office was obliged to reveal for the first time that it held 8,800 files containing the official records of the United Kingdom's former colonies, some of which were highly incriminating. It was denied that the files existed, but they were found at Hanslope Park in Buckinghamshire. The site, owned by the Foreign Office, was unknown to most historians. A photographer sent to photograph the site was detained by the police.[72] It was reported that hidden files were regarded as a guilty secret and hidden according to a damning Foreign Office internal review.[73]

It subsequently transpired that the Foreign Office not only held the 8,800 files at Hanslope Park, but it also held an estimated 1.2 million secret files, referred to as the 'Special Collections', relating to events going back to 1662.[74]

It is possible that the Foreign Office holds the vast photographic archive at Hanslope Park or at some other secret depository. However, it is also possible that the photographs ended up not at the Foreign Office but at the War Office. This is because the War Office despatched Royal Engineer photographers to British Museum excavations and worldwide, and incurred expenditure on photographic apparatus and chemicals. Therefore, the photographs may be held by the Ministry of Defence nowadays.

---

[71] See, for example, letter from A. Panizzi to Earl of Shelburne, 14 November 1857. TNA, FO 78/1335, p. 252. The trail of the photographs ends at the Foreign Office.

[72] Ben Macintyre, 'Archive at "spook central" had secret Mau Mau files', *The Times*, 8 April 2011, p. 10.

[73] Ben Macintyre, 'Embarrassing colonial files hidden for years were Foreign Office's "guilty secret"', *The Times*, 6 May 2011, p. 20.

[74] Ian Cobain, *The History Thieves* (London: Portobello, 2016) p. 137.

In 2013, Ian Cobain, an investigative journalist, discovered that the Ministry of Defence had a large secret depository at Swadlincote in Derbyshire where it leases two large warehouses.[75] He was not permitted access, but an archivist described the depository as resembling the closing scene in the film *Raiders of the Lost Ark*, save that the Ministry of Defence had two such warehouses.[76]

There exists in England a secret depository with photographs and negatives not confined to the photographs taken at excavations. The depository will hold *millions* of photographs taken all over the world by the *hundreds* of Royal Engineers who, from 1858, were under orders to take photographs that would be *'permanently recorded* at the War Department' [emphasis added].[77]

'Permanently recorded' is massive. It means there exists a previously unknown, undocumented resource of photographs taken all over the globe. The photographs will be of interest not only to historians and scholars but to peoples worldwide.

* * *

It has never been appreciated that the tons of antiquities taken under the directions of the trustees of the British Museum were photographed in situ before being removed. The photographs are clearly incriminating, and so it was inevitable they would be buried. But now that the truth is known, the photographs should be put in the public domain. The photographs will reveal wonders not limited to the juxtaposition of monuments, entrances, statues and inscriptions.

---

[75] Cobain, *The History Thieves*, p. 150.
[76] Cobain, *The History Thieves*, p. 151.
[77] Fifth Report of the Science and Art Department of the Committee of Council on Education, UK PP 1857–8 [2385], pp.85–6.

CHAPTER 24

Awards and Rewards

The following individuals took antiquities on behalf of the British Museum and received knighthoods: Alfred Biliotti (Rhodes and Bodrum); Charles Fellows (Xanthus); Austen Henry Layard (Assyria and Babylon); Charles Newton (Branchidae, Cnidus, Cyprus, Ephesus, Halicarnassus, Kalymna, Kaos, Kos, Mytilene, Priene and Rhodes); Henry Creswicke Rawlinson (Assyria and Babylon); and Robert Murdoch Smith (Halicarnassus and Cyrene).

The following individuals took antiquities on behalf of the British Museum and were paid gratuities in addition to salaries: Robert Murdoch Smith R.E. (Halicarnassus and Cyrene) and Edwin A. Porcher R.N. (Cyrene and Carthage), a gratuity of £200 each, a considerable sum at the time, by the 'grateful Trustees of the British Museum';[1] Arthur H. Smith (Cyprus), a gratuity of £200;[2] Hormuzd Rassam (Assyria and Babylon), a gratuity of £400;[3] Charles Newton (for Bodrum), a gratuity of £500.[4]

John Turtle Wood (Ephesus) took antiquities on behalf of the British Museum and was granted an annual pension by Queen Victoria on the recommendation of the prime minister (a trustee of the museum) 'in recognition of his labours at Ephesus'.[5]

---

[1] Wilson, *The British Museum: A History*, p. 362n45.
[2] TNA, T 1/16412.
[3] TNA, T 1/16412.
[4] TNA, FO 78/1491, p. 261.
[5] 'The Discoveries at Ephesus', *The Times*, 27 February 1875, p. 5.

The following all took antiquities on behalf of the British
Museum and received salaries, but do not appear to have been
granted any awards or rewards: Nathan Davis (Carthage);
Consul Dennis (Cyrene, Sicily and Turkey); Consul Guarracino
(Crete); Consul Rogers (Mount Aaron); and Ohnefalsch-
Richter (Cyprus).

R. P. Pullan (Halicarnassus and Priene) received a fixed
contractual payment by the British Museum.

CHAPTER 25

A Museum for the World

In 2003, Neil MacGregor, the then Director of the museum, described the British Museum as an astonishing place because it was the only place in the world where you could see all the world's cultures under one roof.[1] Even more astounding is the truth about how all the world's cultures come to be under one roof in Bloomsbury.

MacGregor praises 'scholars and collectors', as many others have done before him, for collecting from all over the world.[2] However, the museum collections consist of eight million objects, and the resources needed to collect them were beyond those of scholars and collectors.

Credit for the museum collections is due to the following:
- the Foreign Office for appointing Consuls (Newton, Biliotti, Dennis, Guarracino, Rassam and Rogers) to excavate on behalf of the museum;
- the Treasury for unfailingly funding every excavation proposed by the trustees over a period spanning six decades;
- the Admiralty for transporting over one thousand cases containing tons of antiquities and for providing marines to excavate them;
- the War Department for making Royal Engineers available to photograph and dismantle temples and

---

[1] Neil MacGregor, Preface to *Enlightenment: Discovering the World in the Eighteenth Century*. Eds Kim Sloan with Andrew Burnett (London: British Museum Press, 2003), p. 7.

[2] MacGregor, Preface to *Enlightenment: Discovering the World in the Eighteenth Century*, p. 7.

ancient monuments with stone-cutting saws and, on one occasion, gunpowder;
- the soldiers in the British Army for looting as they were encouraged and rewarded to do by Britain's Prize Laws;[3] and
- the trustees of the British Museum (the Establishment) for employing individuals to take whatever the trustees fancied.

It needs to be restated that the following was taken under the directions of the trustees:
- over 500 cases from Assyria;
- 385 cases and 160 blocks of marble from Halicarnassus, Cnidus and Branchidae;
- 110 cases of marble from the Temple of Athena Polias Priene;
- 103 cases from Cyrene;
- in excess of 100 cases of marble from the Temple of Diana at Ephesus;
- 93 cases of mosaics and marble from Carthage;
- 82 cases of marble from Xanthus;
- the contents of over a thousand tombs in Sicily, Rhodes, Sardis, Crete, Benghazi and Cyprus;
- objects from the Holy Land;
- Abyssinian treasures (by the museum's employee); and
- Chinese imperial treasures (by the trustee who ordered the destruction of the Summer Palace).

Between 1840 and 1900, a period of only sixty years, layers upon layers of cultural heritage, laid down over a period of nearly *three hundred centuries*, was taken by the trustees of the museum. It is indeed astonishing that you can see all the world's cultures under one roof. The way it came to be there is beyond comprehension, and it is shameful.

The destruction of the remains of the Assyrian, Babylonian and classical world was not a price worth paying to have on display under one roof one per cent of what the trustees took, with ninety-nine per cent buried in storage.

---

[3] For an explanation of Britain's Prize Laws see Lewis, *China's Summer Palace*, Chapter 6. The British Museum and Prize Agents appeared on the same page of *The British Imperial Calendar.*

* * *

In April 2018, Hartwig Fischer, Director of the museum, revealed plans for an extensive revamp of the museum. In response to a question about nations demanding the return of their objects, he stated that the museum would be bringing a much greater sense of self-scrutiny to its displays: 'The museum has to be completely open about this – that's the first duty'.[4]

Six months after Fischer's statement about being 'completely open', a museum spokeswoman was quoted as saying, 'We are very much in favour of more transparency around the provenance of objects in museum collections'.[5] There should not be 'more' transparency; there must be complete transparency.

In furtherance of Fischer's stated aim, the following four steps should be taken:

   (1) All objects in the collections should be exhibited honestly and transparently. This means correcting all misrepresentations in display labels and in the museum's online database.

   (2) The provenance of all objects taken under directions of the trustees and/or the Foreign Office should be designated as such, this to distinguish them from objects acquired by the trustees in the open market or donated to the museum.

   (3) *All* the photographs (taken at excavations discussed in Chapter 23) should be put in the public domain without any exceptions.

   (4) A second *Royal Commission on the British Museum* should be set up (the first was in 1847). This should investigate how the collections were formed and what to do with them. Clearly ninety-nine per cent of the collections cannot remain in storage in perpetuity while the museum moves to exhibiting trophies in the collections surrounded by an increasing number of retail outlets.

---

[4] Charlotte Higgins, 'Director of the British Museum, Hartwig Fisher, reveals plans for an extensive revamp, but won't be drawn on calls to return plundered works', *The Guardian*, 14 April 2018, pp. 6–7.

[5] David Sanderson and Adam Sage, 'Britain sends treasures back to Africa', *The Times*, 22 November 2018, p. 3.

The notion that it is right that nearly eight million objects, the overwhelming majority of which have absolutely no connection at all to Britain's cultural heritage, should be kept in storage forevermore is plainly wrong.

One part of the solution would be for the British Museum to become a museum *for the world* by establishing satellite museums worldwide. If the museum established fifty satellite museums, each with 49,000 objects (the number Fischer proposes to exhibit in London), it would still hold *seventy* per cent of the collections in storage.

Other museums have set a precedent. In 2007, the Louvre opened an outpost in Abu Dhabi.[6] In 2018, the Victoria and Albert Museum opened a museum in Dundee. There is no reason for the British Museum to remain entrenched in London.

* * *

In 1816 parliament debated whether to grant money to the British Museum to enable it to buy the marble sculptures that had been taken from the Parthenon by the 7th Lord Elgin, known as the Elgin Marbles.

Parliamentary debates spanning more than two hundred years are available online, with the exception of two years, one of which is 1816. As explained in *The Mortgage on the Elgin Marbles*,[7] there was outrage, at the time, in the House of Commons that Elgin had taken the sculptures. He was *hammered* by members of parliament. One member said, 'we should not place in our museum a monument of our disgrace'; another 'could not agree that they had been acquired consistently with the strict rules of morality'.

In the Marbles Debate only two members out of the 112 members who voted on the motion spoke in support of Elgin's action.[8] Despite the condemnation, parliament granted the museum the money. This was only because, if parliament had not done so, the sculptures may have been sold to the Louvre. The thought of the Parthenon Sculptures going to the French, defeated at the Battle of Waterloo twelve months earlier, was unpalatable.

---

[6] Adam Sage, 'Louvre unveils €1bn Abu Dhabi outpost', *The Times*, 7 September 2007, p. 37.

[7] O.M. Lewis, *The Mortgage on the Elgin Marbles* (London: High Tile Books, 2016).

[8] Elgin Marbles, HC Deb, 7 June 1816, vol. 34, col. 1028.

It was not only in parliament that Elgin took a hammering. Lord Byron savaged Elgin in his poem *Childe Harold's Pilgrimage*, accusing him of being another Verres, a Roman magistrate who governed Sicily. In 70 BC, Verres was charged with stealing art from Sicily and prosecuted by Cicero.

Times and morals change. In 1816, members of parliament, Byron and many others believed it was morally wrong to take whatever you fancied from other countries. But by 1867, a British Consul (George Dennis) was appointed to Sicily specifically to rob tombs for the British Museum.

> To steal a nation's antiquities is to rob its people of their history, heritage and identity.[9]

These words, from an editorial in *The Times*, pointed the finger at 'grave-robbers, church vandals and rogue archaeologists'. This book points the finger firmly at the trustees of the British Museum who, between 1840 and 1900, were megalomaniacal hoarders.

---

[9] 'Preventing Profit from Plunder', *The Times*, 7 May 2018, p. 29.

CHAPTER 26

The Key

'Stowing away cases for British Museum.'
HMS *Supply* log book entry.[10]

Entries in HM Ship log books record the places and dates that antiquities were stowed on board. With a fixed date and location it is possible to uncover who was excavating there, how the excavations were funded and what antiquities were taken.

However, finding entries, as the one above, in an HMS log book is like finding a needle in a haystack. This is because at the time there were 735 HM Ships in the Royal Navy (in the quarterly *Navy List*) and each ship kept a monthly log. Therefore, in the three decades between 1840 and 1870, there are in excess of 260,000 log books with manuscript entries covering nearly eight million days. Research on this book covers HM Ships that transported antiquities for the British Museum over six decades, 1840–1900.

The correspondence between the Admiralty and the trustees of the British Museum between 1840 and 1900 would reveal the HM Ships that transported antiquities for the museum. However, most Admiralty files covering this period have been destroyed; little survives at The National Archives.

But The National Archives does hold three other invaluable sources: the Admiralty Digests from 1793 to 1974, the Admiralty Index, and the original HM Ship log books.

In Digests the Admiralty recorded the substance of every letter sent and received. In the Index the Admiralty recorded the sailing instructions issued to all HM Ships (the Index

---

[10] TNA, ADM 53/6598.

served other purposes, but it enabled the Admiralty to keep track of HM Ships). Little went unrecorded by the Admiralty in the Digest and Index. An example of the detail recorded is an Index entry for the troop ship HMS *Serapis*, 'Issue of lemon juice to troops'.[11]

The log books contain full nautical records of each ship's voyage. The voyages correlate with directions recorded in the Index.

* * *

In the Digest, correspondence was recorded under headings called 'Cuts' or 'Cases'. In 1843, the Digest contained 104 headings with 360 sub-headings. Digests are large leather-bound volumes (50cm x 36cm x 10cm) and there can be eight volumes for a single year.

The following is an example of entries in the 1858 Digest. The Admiralty recorded that Lord Malmesbury (the Foreign Secretary) reported that forty cases of Carthaginian antiquities were ready for shipment at Tunis and that HMS *Supply*, returning home from Bodrum with antiquities, should sail to Tunis to collect them.[12]

In the Index (large leather-bound volumes, 50cm x 36cm x 10cm) the Admiralty recorded that *Supply* was ordered to Tunis in February 1858.[13]

The entries in the Digest and Index pinpoint *the month* that a named HM Ship transported antiquities for the British Museum. However, to pinpoint a log book you must first find entries in the Digest which name HM Ships that transported not only antiquities but did so specifically for the British Museum.

The National Archives has a useful aid for researchers, the *Combined Alphabetical Index to Admiralty Digest Headings Used in 1800, 1843, 1909 and 1963*. The majority of headings in the Digest are to be expected; for example, the headings cover dockyards, ships, seamen, naval stores, etc. An unexpected heading is Case 59.8 Projects for Annoying the Enemy.

Prior to 1844, the Admiralty did not dedicate a specific heading to the British Museum. It recorded correspondence

---

[11] Admiralty Index 1869. TNA, ADM 12/826.
[12] Case 90a British Museum. TNA, ADM 12/657.
[13] Index S–T. TNA, ADM 12/648.

with the museum under various cases, one being Case 72.6, Freightage of Treasure. Therefore, everything recorded by the Admiralty with regard to transporting the Xanthian Marbles, for example, is recorded under Case 72.6.

The British Museum is not in a heading in the *Combined Alphabetical Index to Admiralty Digest Headings*. However, knowing that the trustees of the museum corresponded with the Admiralty, it was a matter of turning the pages of eight volumes of an annual Digest (with 104 headings and 360 sub-headings) to discover that after 1844 *all* correspondence with the British Museum was recorded under Case 90a 'British Museum & Scientific Subjects'.

In the *Combined Alphabetical Index to Admiralty Digest Headings*, the heading of Case 90a is 'Scientific Subjects'. This was correct in 1843, but in 1844 it was changed to 'British Museum and Scientific Subjects'. This is the heading used in the leather-bound Digests.

Case 90a is therefore the key. It is cited in over thirty of the footnotes in this book. It is the bedrock of The National Archives references (ADM 12) in Appendix 2, 'Antiquities transported by HM Ships 1839–1891'. Case 90a identifies the HM Ships that transported antiquities for the British Museum. It specifies the locations and the dates. Case 90a makes it possible to pinpoint the monthly log books of the fifty HM Ships listed in Chapter 4. Case 90a unlocks the truth about how the trustees of the British Museum took antiquities.

Everything in this book relating to the transportation of antiquities by HM Ships is founded on three unimpeachable primary sources – the Admiralty Digest, the Admiralty Index and the original HM Ship log books.

Appendices

Appendix 1: Expenditure on taking antiquities for the British Museum, 1842–1900

		£
1842	'Freight and carriage,... marbles from **Xanthus**'[1]	1,012
	'... to make further excavations in search of marbles at **Xanthus**.'[2]	1,000
1843	'Expenses incurred by the Admiralty in the conveyance of **Xanthian** marbles in 1842–43.'[13]	356
1844	'Expenses of excavations at **Xanthus**, and conveying sculptures to England.'[4]	1,000
	'Credit ... for expenses of the **Xanthian** Antiquities.'[5]	6,217
1845	'Expenses incurred in collecting and conveying to England the **Xanthian** antiquities.'[6]	1,387
	'Expense of **Canning Marbles and Assyrian** antiquities in the **Kurdistan**.'[7]	unspecified
1847	'Received on account of grant for the removal of marbles from **Bodrum**.'[8]	352
	'Received on account of grant for excavations etc., in **Kurdistan** and transport of marbles.'[9]	2,800
	'Antiquities from **Nimroud** removal of.'[10]	unspecified
1848	'Received on account of grant for excavations etc., in **Assyria**, and transport of marbles.'[11]	500
	'**Assyria** ... to carry on researches in.'[12]	3,000
	'**Mr. Layard**, for removal of antiquities discovered by him at and near **Nineveh**.'[13]	unspecified

---

1 Account of Income and Expenditure of British Museum, 1842. UK PP, paper no. 106, p. 2.
2 Registers of Papers, British Museum, 1843. TNA, T 2/182.
3 Account of Income and Expenditure of British Museum, 1843. UK PP, paper no. 116, p. 2.
4 Account of Income and Expenditure of British Museum, 1844. UK PP, paper no. 287, p. 4.
5 Registers of Papers, British Museum, 1845. TNA, T 2/190.
6 Account of Income and Expenditure of British Museum, 1845. UK PP, paper no. 151, p. 4.
7 Registers of Papers, British Museum, 1846. TNA, T 2/194.
8 Account of Income and Expenditure of British Museum, 1847. UK PP, paper no. 139, p. 4.
9 Account of Income and Expenditure of British Museum, 1847. UK PP, paper no. 139, p. 4.
10 Registers of Papers. British Museum, 1847. TNA, T 2/198.
11 Account of Income and Expenditure of British Museum, 1848. UK PP, paper no. 140, p. 4.
12 Registers of Papers. British Museum, 1849. TNA, T 2/206.
13 Registers of Papers. British Museum, 1849. TNA, T 2/206.

	'Received on account of grant for excavating etc., in **Assyria** and transport of marbles.'[14]	1,500
	'Received on account of grant for excavations etc., in **Assyria**, and transport of marbles.'[15]	2,003
	'To defray expenses incurred by the **Assyrian** Expedition under the direction of **Mr. Layard**, in excavations.'[16]	3,500
	'**Colonel Rawlinson** antiquarian researches in **Asia Minor**.'[17]	500
	'... expenditure for excavations etc., in **Assyria**, and transport of marbles.'[18]	3,087
	'To discharge actual expenses incurred by **Mr. Layard** in **Assyria** over and above the sum voted by Parliament.'[19]	1,466
	'For researches in **Assyria** and **Babylonia** under the direction of **Lieutenant Colonel Rawlinson**.'[20]	1,500
1853	'Excavations etc., in **Assyria**, and transport of marbles under **A.H. Layard**.'[21]	1,973
	'Excavations etc., in **Assyria**, and transport of marbles under **Colonel Rawlinson**.'[22]	756
	'Credits ... researches in **Assyria** and **Babylon**.'[23]	1,500
1854	'Excavations etc., in **Assyria**, and transport of marbles under **Colonel Rawlinson**.'[24]	1,112
	'Expenses ... transmission ... of marbles ... discovered at **Kuyunjik** in **Assyria** and for carrying further excavations.'[25]	1,500
1855	'Excavations etc., in **Assyria**, and transport of marbles under **Colonel Rawlinson**.'[26]	2,451
	'**Assyrian** antiquities. For delivery of a collection from Bombay.'[27]	unspecified

14 Account of Income and Expenditure of British Museum, 1849. UK PP, paper no. 196, p. 2.

15 Account of Income and Expenditure of British Museum, 1850. UK PP, paper no. 68, p. 4.

16 Public works and buildings. Estimates etc., for 1851–52. UK PP, 211-I-VII, p. 24.

17 Registers of Papers, British Museum, 1851. TNA, T 2/214.

18 Account of Receipt and Expenditure, Special Purchases of British Museum for the year ending 31 March 1852. UK PP, 312, p. 5.

19 Public works and buildings. Estimates etc., for 1851–52. UK PP, 238-I-VII, p. 39.

20 Public works and buildings. Estimates etc., for 1851–52. UK PP, 238-I-VII, p. 39.

21 Account of Income and Expenditure of British Museum, 1853. UK PP, paper no. 319, p. 3.

22 Account of Income and Expenditure of British Museum, 1853. UK PP, paper no. 319, p. 3.

23 Registers of Papers, British Museum, 1853. TNA, T 2/222.

24 Account of Income and Expenditure of British Museum, 1854. UK PP, paper no. 176, p. 3.

25 Public works and buildings. Estimates etc., for 1855. UK PP, 172-I-VII, p. 38.

26 Account of Income and Expenditure of British Museum, 1855. UK PP, paper no. 184, p. 3.

27 Registers of Papers, British Museum, 1855. TNA T 2/230.

1856 'Excavations, etc., in Assyria, and transport of marbles under **Colonel Sir H. C. Rawlinson.**'[28]	882
'Assyrian Sculptures from Basra – for delivery of.'[29]	unspecified
'Vases and antiquities from **Tripoli** [Cyrene]. For delivery of 19 cases.'[30]	unspecified
Excavations at **Carthage.**[31]	200
'Antiquities for delivery of 52 cases shipped.'[32]	unspecified
'Antiquities for delivery of 28 cases.'[33]	unspecified
1857 'cost of the excavations ... by **Vice-Consul Newton** at **Bodrum** and for conveyance to the Museum of the marbles.'[34]	5,000
'For mosaics from **Tunis** [Carthage]. For delivery of certain cases.'[35]	unspecified
'Excavations ... **Carthage** ... expenses including salary for **N. Davis.**'[36]	984
'**Bodrum** ... to repay **Lord Clarendon** the sum of £3,133.'[37]	3,133
Excavations at **Carthage** ... expenses including salary for **N. Davis.**[38]	1,080
1859 Excavations at **Carthage** ... expenses including salary for **N. Davis.**[39]	592
'for a continuation of the excavations at **Bodrum** (Halicarnassus).'[40]	2,000
1860 'For delivery of antiquities from **Carthage.**'[41]	unspecified

---

28 Account of Income and Expenditure of British Museum, 1856. UK PP, paper no. 147, p. 3.

29 Registers of Papers, British Museum, 1856. TNA T 2/234.

30 Registers of Papers, 1856. British Museum, 1856. TNA T 2/234.

31 Foreign Office: Letters and receipts from N. Davis (Carthaginian excavations), 1856–1860. TNA, FO 335/110.

32 Registers of Papers, 1856. British Museum. TNA, T 2/234.

33 Registers of Papers, 1856. British Museum. TNA, T 2/234.

34 Estimates etc., for Civil Services, 1857–58. UK PP, paper no.162-I-VII, p. 29.

35 Registers of Papers, 1857. British Museum. TNA T 2/238.

36 Foreign Office: Letters and receipts from N. Davis (Carthaginian excavations), 1856–1860. TNA, FO 335/110.

37 From C.E. Trevelyan to E. Hammond, 1 March 1858. Treasury: Out-Letters to the Foreign Office. TNA, T 12/1.

38 Foreign Office: Letters and receipts from N. Davis (Carthaginian excavations), 1856–1860. TNA, FO 335/110.

39 Foreign Office: Letters and receipts from N. Davis (Carthaginian excavations), 1856–1860. TNA, FO 335/110.

40 Estimates etc., for Civil Services, 1860. UK PP, paper no. 58-I-VII, p. 34.

41 Registers of Papers, 1860. British Museum. TNA, T 2/250.

		Amount
	Excavations at Carthage including salary to **N. Davis**.[42]	287
	'amount of supplies issued by the Naval Department to the **Bodrum** Expedition.'[43]	644
	'amount of stores supplied by the War Department to the **Bodrum** Expedition.'[44]	771
	'to **Mr. Newton** … expenses connected with the **Bodrum** Expedition.'[45]	103
	'to the War Department … pay … Royal Engineers under **Lt. Smith** … **Bodrum** Expedition.'[46]	592
1861	'**Bodrum** Expedition … expenditure has been repaid.'[47]	270
	'**Cyrenaica** [Cyrene] antiquities from. delivery of 24 cases unopened.'[48]	unspecified
1862	'Expenditure … in connection with the excavations at **Bodrum, Cnidus**, etc.'[49]	309
	'Excavations in the **Cyrenaica** [Cyrene] under **Lieutenant Smith R.E. and Porcher R.N.**'[50]	1,323
	'**Assyrian** marble slabs found in **Armenia**. Expenses of bringing to London.'[51]	unspecified
	'Excavations at **Bodrum, Cnidus** etc.'[52]	311
	'Excavations in the **Cyrenaica** [Cyrene] under **Lieutenant Smith R.E. and Porcher R.N.**'[53]	1,500
	'**Babylon** – excavations near, for grant of.'[54]	500
1864	'Excavations in **Babylonia**, under the superintendence of **Colonel Kemball** [Consul at Bagdad].'[55]	500

---

42 Foreign Office: Letters and receipts from N. Davis (Carthaginian excavations), 1856–1860. TNA, FO 335/110.

43 From G. Hamilton to E. Hammond, 4 March 1860. Treasury: Out-Letters to Foreign Office. TNA, T 12/2.

44 From G. Hamilton to E. Hammond, 4 March 1860. Treasury: Out-Letters to Foreign Office. TNA, T 12/2.

45 From G. Hamilton to E. Hammond, 4 March 1860. Treasury: Out-Letters to Foreign Office. TNA, T 12/2.

46 From G. Hamilton to E. Hammond, 4 March 1860. Treasury: Out-Letters to Foreign Office. TNA, T 12/2.

47 Registers of Papers, 1861. British Museum. TNA, T 2/254.

48 Registers of Papers, 1861. British Museum. TNA, T 2/254.

49 Account of Income and Expenditure of British Museum. 1862. UK PP, paper no. 200, p. 3.

50 Account of Income and Expenditure of British Museum. 1862. UK PP, paper no. 200, p. 3.

51 Registers of Papers, 1862. British Museum. TNA, T 2/258.

52 Estimates for Civil Services, 1863. UK PP, paper no.112-I-VII, p. 33.

53 Estimates for Civil Services, 1863. UK PP, paper no.112-I-VII, p. 33.

54 Registers of Papers, 1864. British Museum. TNA, T 2/262.

55 Estimates for Civil Services, 1864–5. UK PP, paper no.103-I-VII, p. 37.

Year	Description	Amount
1866	'Antiquities for delivery of 32 cases in HMS *Supply*.'[56]	unspecified
1867	'Further excavations at **Bodrum**, under the superintendence of **Mr. Vice-Consul Biliotti**.'[57]	2,000
	'Further excavations at **Bodrum**, under the superintendence of **Mr. Vice-Consul Biliotti**.'[58]	1,374
1868	'Application from **Trustees of British Museum** … excavations in **Asia Minor** under **George Dennis**.'[59]	500
	'paid for **Mr. Wood's** passage to continue excavations at **Ephesus** and … advances for the excavations.'[60]	830
	'Amount in the hands of **Vice-Consul Dennis** for explorations in Asia Minor.'[61]	214
	'Amount in the hands of **Mr. Consul Rogers** for excavations in the **Hauran** [Mount Aaron].'[62]	30
	'For excavations in **Asia Minor** under the superintendence of **Mr. George Dennis** Vice-Consul at Benghazi.'[63]	500
	'**Ephesus** excavations at. For authority to issue a further.'[64]	600
1869	'**British Museum** … removal from **Smyrna** certain antiquities [from **Priene**] consigned to them.'[65]	unspecified
	Expenditure by **Mr. J. T. Wood** on the excavations at **Ephesus**.'[66]	unspecified
	'**Davis, Mr.** … for his services in carrying on excavations at **Carthage** 1856–59.'[67]	unspecified
	'**Dennis** Vice-Consul engaged … exploring cemeteries in **Asia Minor** [Sardis] … expenses.'[68]	unspecified
	Purchases. Greek and Roman antiquities (including excavations).'[69]	2,500

56 Registers of Papers, 1864. British Museum. TNA T 2/266.
57 Estimates for Civil Services, 1866. UK PP, paper no. 90-I-VII, p. 37.
58 Account of Income and Expenditure of British Museum, 31 March 1866. UK PP, paper no.187, p. 4.
59 From G. Hamilton to E. Hammond, 4 March 1860. Treasury: Out-Letters to the Foreign Office. TNA T 12/4.
60 Account of Income and Expenditure of British Museum, 31 March 1868. UK PP, paper no. 254, p. 3.
61 Account of Income and Expenditure of British Museum, 31 March 1868. UK PP, paper no. 254, p. 3.
62 Account of Income and Expenditure of British Museum, 31 March 1868. UK PP, paper no. 254, p. 3.
63 Account of Income and Expenditure of British Museum, 31 March 1868. UK PP, paper no. 254, p. 3.
64 Registers of Papers, 1869. British Museum. TNA, T 2/2826.
65 Registers of Papers, 1869. British Museum. TNA, T 2/286.
66 Appropriation Accounts of Sums Granted for Civil Services 1868–69, UK PP, paper no. 47, p. 212.
67 Registers of Papers, 1869. British Museum. TNA, T 2/286.
68 Registers of Papers, 1869. British Museum. TNA, T 2/286.
69 Account of Income and Expenditure of British Museum, 31 March 1869. UK PP, paper no. 211, p. 6.

Year		Amount
1871	'Ephesus excavations at. Further for sanction of an additional ...' [70]	1,500
	'Trustees of British Museum ... expenses in connection with the excavations at **Ephesus**.' [71]	47
1872	'**Ephesus. Temple of Diana**. For further advance for excavations.' [72]	unspecified
	'Trustees of the **British Museum** ... expenses in connection with excavations at **Ephesus**.' [73]	121
	'**Ephesus** – excavations at. Recommending grant of £6,000.' [74]	6,000

After 1872, expenditure on British Museum excavations was not shown in the museum's accounts, with exception of Cyprus, but was recorded by the Treasury.

Year		Amount
1874	'**Assyria** – excavations. Gratuity of £200 to **Mr. Smith** [British Museum].' [75]	200
	'Trustees of **British Museum** ... expenses incurred in packing antiquities at **Ephesus**.' [76]	17
1875	'Excavations in **Mesopotamia**. For sanction to expend ... in current year.' [77]	1,000
	'**Ephesus, Temple of Diana** ... employing **Mr. Smith**.' [78]	unspecified
	'**Mesopotamia** excavations. For insertion ... in estimates ...' [79]	2,000
1878	'**Mesopotamia**. Sanction to increase **Mr. H. Rassam** personal allowance whilst employed.' [80]	unspecified
	'**Assyria & Mesopotamia** ... to insert sum of ... in the estimates ...' [81]	3,000

---

70 Registers of Papers, 1871. British Museum. TNA, T 2/294.
71 Registers of Papers, 1872. British Museum. TNA, T 2/298.
72 Navy. Appropriation Account 1872–73. UK PP, paper no. 28, p. 11.
73 Registers of Papers, 1872. British Museum. TNA, T 2/298.
74 Registers of Papers, 1872. British Museum. TNA, T 2/298.
75 Registers of Papers, 1874. British Museum. TNA, T 2/306.
76 Navy. Appropriation Account of Sums granted by Parliament for Navy Services 1873–74. UK PP, paper no. 67, p. 95.
77 Registers of Papers, 1875. British Museum. TNA, T 2/310.
78 Registers of Papers, 1875. British Museum. TNA, T 2/310.
79 Registers of Papers, 1875. British Museum. TNA, T 2/310.
80 Registers of Papers, 1878. British Museum. TNA, T 2/322.
81 Registers of Papers, 1878. British Museum. TNA, T 2/322.

Year	Description	Amount
1879	'Cyprus. For sanction to expenditure of sending out an archaeologist to carry on excavations.'[82]	unspecified
1880	'Cyprus ... proposed explorations for antiquities ... for authority to expend.'[83]	300
	'Assyria and Mesopotamia ... to be inserted in estimates ... on a/c of excavations for antiquities.'[84]	3,000
	'Assyria and Babylonian ... For sanction to provisions in estimates for re-employment **Mr. Rassam**.'[85]	unspecified
	'Assyria excavations. For sanction to insert £2,500 in estimates.'[86]	2,500
	'For prosecuting excavations on the site of the **City of Sardis**.'[87]	2,000
1882	'Assyrian and Babylonian excavation. Gratuity to **Mr. Rassam**.'[88]	400
	'Babylonian and Assyrian excavations. For sanction to insert £2,500 in estimates.'[89]	2,500
	'To insert £2,000 in the estimates for excavations on the site of the City of **Sardis**.'[90]	2,000
1883	'**Mr. Rassam** for payment of £200 to ...'[91]	200
1884	'**Temple of Diana at Ephesus**. For sanction to purchase of ground adjoining the site ...'[92]	unspecified
1885	'Excavations at **Sardis**. For grant to **Mr. Dennis** HM Consul in order to undertake.'[93]	unspecified
1886	'**Cyprus**. Expenditure in connection with excavations for antiquities.'[94]	unspecified
1887	'**Cyprus** excavations. To insert £100 in estimates for.'[95]	100

82 Registers of Papers, 1878. British Museum. TNA, T 2/322.
83 Registers of Papers, 1879. British Museum. TNA, T 2/326.
84 Registers of Papers, 1879. British Museum. TNA, T 2/326.
85 Registers of Papers, 1880. British Museum. TNA, T 2/330.
86 Registers of Papers, 1881. British Museum. TNA, T 2/334.
87 Registers of Papers, 1881. British Museum. TNA, T 2/334.
88 Registers of Papers, 1882. British Museum. TNA, T 2/338.
89 Registers of Papers, 1882. British Museum. TNA, T 2/338.
90 Registers of Papers, 1882. British Museum. TNA, T 2/338.
91 Registers of Papers, 1883. British Museum. TNA, T 2/342.
92 Registers of Papers, 1884. British Museum. TNA, T 2/346.
93 Registers of Papers, 1885. British Museum. TNA, T 2/350.
94 Registers of Papers, 1886. British Museum. TNA, T 2/354.
95 Registers of Papers, 1887. British Museum. TNA, T 2/358.

	Persian excavations. For sanction to travelling ... accompanying **Col. Murdoch Smith**.[96]	unspecified
	Statue of Ramases II in **Egypt**. For removal to this country.[97]	unspecified
	'**Assyrian, Babylonian** and **Egyptian** explorations. Proposed mission of **Mr. Budge**.[98]	unspecified
	'**Egypt** and **Babylonian** mission. To expend £400 as necessary ...'[99]	400
1888	'**Kuyunjik** and **Sippara**. To resume excavations at ...'[100]	unspecified
	Egypt and **Babylonia**. Excavations at **Honorarium** to **Mr. Budge** for his expenses.'[101]	unspecified
1894	'excavations ... in the Island of **Cyprus** [Turner Bequest].'[102]	531
1895	'excavations ... in the Island of **Cyprus** [Turner Bequest].'[103]	305
1896	'excavations ... in the Island of **Cyprus** [Turner Bequest].'[104]	331
1898	'excavations ... in the Island of **Cyprus** [Turner Bequest].'[105]	16
	'**Cyprus** excavations. To expend £500 out of [British Museum] Purchase grant.'[106]	500
1898	'**Cyprus** ... resumption of excavations on the **Tekké** site near Larnaca.'[107]	unspecified
1899	'**Cyprus** excavations. Diversion of expense on a/c of.'[108]	unspecified

96 Registers of Papers, 1887. British Museum. TNA, T 2/358.
97 Registers of Papers, 1887. British Museum. TNA, T 2/358.
98 Registers of Papers, 1887. British Museum. TNA, T 2/358.
99 Registers of Papers, 1887. British Museum. TNA, T 2/358.
100 Registers of Papers, 1888. British Museum. TNA, T 2/362.
101 Registers of Papers, 1891. British Museum. TNA, T 2/374.
102 Account of Income and Expenditure of British Museum, 31 March 1894. UK PP, paper no. 281, p. 9.
103 Account of Income and Expenditure of British Museum, 31 March 1895. UK PP, paper no. 353, p. 9.
104 Account of Income and Expenditure of British Museum, 31 March 1896. UK PP, paper no. 258, p. 9.
105 Account of Income and Expenditure of British Museum, 31 March 1898. UK PP, paper no. 174, p. 9.
106 Registers of Papers, 1897. British Museum, TNA, T 2/398.
107 Registers of Papers, 1898. British Museum, TNA, T 2/402.
108 Registers of Papers, 1899. British Museum, TNA, T 2/406.

Appendix 2: Antiquities transported by HM Ships, 1839–91

Sources: The National Archives references: ADM 12 Admiralty Digest (Case 90a British Museum); ADM 12 Admiralty Index (HM Ship); ADM 53 HM Ship log book; ADM 54 HM Ship Master's log; T 2 Treasury: Registers of Papers; T 11 Treasury: Books of Out-Letters of Customs and Excise.

Notes:

- Malta was a transshipment hub for antiquities;
- Assyrian antiquities were also transported by merchant ships. For example, in 1852 *Apprentice* (a merchant ship) transported Assyrian antiquities from Basra to London.[1]

	Year	Antiquities	Place	HM SHIP	The National Archives reference
1.	1839	Sphinx	Alexandria	*Megaera*	ADM 12/360 & ADM 12/353
2.	1839	Sphinx (the above)	Malta	*Talavera*	ADM 12/360 & ADM 12/355
3.	1842	Marbles (78 cases)	Xanthus	*Medea*	ADM 53/899
4.	1842	Marbles (the above 78 cases)	Malta	*Cambridge*	ADM 53/306 & ADM 12/400
5.	1842	Sphinx	unknown	*Talavera*	ADM 12/400
6.	1844	Marbles (5 cases)	Xanthus	*Warspite*	ADM 54/315 & ADM 12/425
7.	1844	Marbles (the 5 above)	Malta	*Vesuvius*	ADM 53/1510 & ADM 12/425
8.	1845	Greek antiquities (17 cases)	Athens	*Apollo*	ADM 12/ 449 & ADM 12/434
9.	1845	Greek antiquities	Malta	*Belvidera*	ADM 12/ 449 & ADM 12/434
10.	1846	Marbles (16 packages)	Bodrum	*Siren*	ADM 53/3229 & ADM 12/465
11.	1846	Marbles (the above)	Malta	*Acheron*	ADM 12/465
12.	1848	Assyrian antiquities (55 cases)	Nineveh	*Jumna*	ADM 53/2711 & ADM 12/497
13.	1848	Sculptured stone	Malta	*Fantome*	ADM 12/497 & ADM 12/484

[1] Case 90a British Museum. TNA ADM 12/512.

14.	1849	Assyrian antiquities	Nineveh	*Meeanee*	ADM 12/512 & ADM 12/502
15.	1855	Four cases antiquities	Mytilene	unknown	T 11/110
16.	1856	Antiquities (28 cases)	Malta	*Perseverance*	ADM 12/615 & T 11/110
17.	1856	Antiquities (19 Cases)	Tripoli	unknown	T 2/234
18.	1856	Sculptures (36 cases)	Kertch (Crimea)	*W.S. Lindsay*[2]	T 11/110 & T 2/234
19.	1856	Assyrian sculptures (78 cases)	Nineveh	*Christiana Carnel*[3]	T 11/110
20.	1856	Assyrian sculptures (49 cases)	Nineveh	*Manuel*[4]	T 11/110
21.	1857	Marbles & Mosaics (218 cases)	Bodrum	*Gorgon*	ADM 53/5759 & ADM 12/640
22.	1857	Female statue	Smyrna	*Supply*	ADM 53/6598 & FO 78/1334
23.	1857	Mosaics & antiquities (39 cases)	Carthage	*Curacoa*	ADM 53/5829 & ADM 12/640
24.	1858	Marbles 160 cases, 160 blocks	Bodrum and Carthage*	*Supply*	ADM 12/657 & ADM 53/6598&9
25.	1859	Antiquities (55 cases)	Bodrum and Rhodes	*Supply*	ADM 12/672 & ADM 53/6600
26.	1860	Antiquities (20 cases)	Carthage	*Supply*	ADM 12/689 & T 2/250
27.	1860	Marble 4 figs & 1 horse	Carthage	*Kertch*	FO 335/110 & ADM 53/8783
28.	1861	Antiquities	Cyrene	*Assurance*	ADM 53/7012 & ADM 12/705
29.	1861	Antiquities	Carthage	*Caradoc*	ADM 12/ 691 & ADM 1/5777
30.	1861	Antiquities (63 cases)	Cyrene	*Melpomene*	ADM 12/705 & ADM 53/7575
31.	1861	Antiquities	Crete & Cyrene	*Scourge*	ADM 12/705 & ADM 12/696
32.	1861	Antiquities (22 cases)	Cyrene	*Supply*	ADM 12/705 & ADM 1/5777
33.	1861	Antiquities (65 cases)	Bodrum	*Supply*	ADM 53/8387, T2/254
34.	1861	Two sarcophagi	Crete	*Medina*	ADM 53/7763 & ADM 12/705
35.	1862	Antiquities	Crete	*Scourge*	ADM 12/720 & ADM 12/712
36.	1862	Antiquities	Athens & Corfu	*Algiers*	ADM 12/720 & ADM 12/706
37.	1863	Antiquities	Mount Aaron, Petra	*Phoebe*	ADM 12/736 & ADM 12/727
38.	1863	Marble torso	Elea	*Medina*	ADM 12/736 & ADM 12/726
39.	1864	Antiquities	Rhodes	*Chanticleer*	ADM 53/8459 & ADM 12/ 753

[2] *W.S. Lindsay* chartered by Admiralty (NA WO 28/156).
[3] *Christiana Carnel* chartered by Admiralty (T 11/110).
[4] *Manuel* chartered by Admiralty (T 11/110).

No.	Year	Description	Location	Ship	References
40.	1864	Antiquities (32 Cases)	Rhodes	*Supply*	ADM 12/753, ADM 12/744
41.	1864	Antiquities	Civita Vecchia	*Foxhound*	ADM 12/753
42.	1865	Antiquities (44 cases)	Bodrum	*Chanticleer*	ADM 53/8460 & ADM 12/768
43.	1866	Antiquities (above 44 cases)	Malta	*Orontes*	ADM 12/768 & ADM 53/8687
44.	1866	Coins and marble pillar	Corfu	*Pelican*	ADM 12/775
45.	1866	Antiquities	Malta	*Industry*	ADM 12/773
46.	1867	Marble statue	Crete	*Wizard*	ADM 12/793
47.	1868	Ancient arms/antiquities	Rhodes & Ephesus	*Terrible*	ADM 53/9346 & ADM 12/809
48.	1869	Antiquities	Beirut	*Rapid*	ADM 12/826 & ADM 12/889
49.	1869	Antiquities (135 cases, 80 tons)	Priene and Ephesus	*Antelope*	ADM 12/835 & ADM 53/9633
50.	1869	Antiquities (part above)	Malta	*Simoom*	ADM 53/9570 &ADM 12/844
51.	1870	Antiquities (part above)	Malta	*Himalaya*	ADM 12/841 & ADM 1/6139
52.	1871	Three boxes	Malta	*Orontes*	ADM 12/865 & ADM 12/901
53.	1872	Marbles (53 cases)	Ephesus	*Caledonia*	ADM 53/9994 & ADM 12/901
54.	1872	Casts (14 cases)	Athens	*Rapid*	ADM 12/889 & ADM 1/6241
55.	1872	Antiquities (13 packages)	Malta	*Agincourt*	ADM 53/10401 & ADM 1/6241
56.	1873	Marbles (31 cases & 16 blocks)	Ephesus	*Swiftsure*	ADM 53/10337 & ADM 12/924
57.	1873	Antiquities (34 cases)	Ephesus	*Tamar*	ADM 12/912 & ADM 12/924
58.	1874	Antiquities (23 cases & 63 blocks)	Ephesus	*Revenge*	ADM 12/947 & ADM 53/10847
59.	1875	Casts from Parthenon (26 cases)	Athens	*Lord Warden*	ADM 12/955 & ADM 12/968
60.	1879	Antiquities	Ierabolis	*Condor*	ADM 12/1030 & ADM 12/1045
61.	1881	Monolith Marbles	Ierabolis	*Monarch*	ADM 12/1069 & ADM 12/1074
62.	1881	Karchemish Monolith	Alexandria	*Hecla*	ADM 53/11598 & ADM 12/1078
63.	1881	Monolith (above)	Malta	*Humber*	ADM 53/12108 & ADM 12/1078
64.	1887	Statue	Thasos	*Sylvia*	ADM 12/1168 & ADM 53/15947
65.	1887	Antiquities	Port Said	*Tyne*	ADM 12/1169 & ADM 53/16371
66.	1891	Sculpture, capital bull Cyprus	Famagusta	*Melita*	ADM 12/1233
67.	1891	Above stone winged bull	Alexandria	*Amphion*	ADM 12/1222 & ADM 53/12454

Appendix 3:
British Museum antiquities in *The Illustrated London News*, 1843–1900[1]

1843

'Xanthian Marbles. British Museum: Exhibition of Marbles from Asia Minor' (11 February 1843, pp. 97–8).
'The Temple of Ephesus' (22 March 1843, p. 282).

1847

'The Budrum Marbles in the British Museum' (30 January 1847, p. 80).
'The Nimroud Sculptures' (26 June 1847, pp. 409, 410 and 412).
'The Nimroud Sculptures at the British Museum – Second Arrival' (28 August 1847, p. 144).

1848

'The Nimroud Sculptures lately received at the British Museum' (16 December 1848, pp. 373–4).
'The Nimroud Sculptures' (30 December 1848, p. 425).

1849

'The Nimroud Sculptures. Just received at the British Museum' (31 March 1849, pp. 213–14)

1850

'The Assyrian Inscriptions' (26 January 1850, p. 55).
'Nimroud Sculptures Just Received at the British Museum' (2 March 1850, pp. 150–2).
'Nimroud Sculptures Just Received at the British Museum' (26 October 1850, p. 332).
'Nimroud Sculptures at the British Museum' (21 December 1850, p. 484).
'Nimroud Sculptures at the British Museum' (28 December 1850, p. 505).

---

[1] A British Library online resource since 2019.

187

1851

'More Nineveh Sculptures' (18 January 1851, p. 45).

'The Cyrene Marbles in the British Museum' (30 November 1861, p. 563).

1852

'Reception of Nineveh Sculptures at the British Museum' (28 February 1852, p. 184).

'Nimroud Antiquities' (29 May 1852, pp. 426–8).

1855

'Antiquities from Kertch' (16 June 1855, p. 597).

'Recent Discoveries at Nineveh' (3 November 1855, pp. 521–2).

1856

'Recent Discoveries at Nineveh' (19 January 1856, pp. 63–4).

'Inscriptions from Nineveh' (26 January 1856, p. 102).

'Ivory Carvings from Nineveh' (12 April 1856, p. 390).

'The British Museum: Additions to the Assyrian Sculptures' (24 May 1956, pp. 553–4).

'Assyrian Sculptures' (16 August 1856, p. 178).

'Nineveh Sculptures' (15 November 1856, p. 502).

'Recent Researches in Babylonia' (27 December 1856, p. 656).

1857

'A Glance at the Zoological Representations on the Nineveh Bas-Reliefs' (10 Jan 1857, p. 28).

'Ruins of Carthage' (14 February 1857, p. 143).

'Sculptures from the Tomb of Mausolus at Halicarnassus' (24 October 1857, pp. 422 and 424).

'The British Museum: Nineveh Sculptures' (21 November 1857, pp. 515–16).

'The British Museum: Nineveh Sculptures' (26 December 1857, pp. 651 and 656).

1858

'Arabs excavating at the Ruins of Carthage' (15 May 1858, p. 480).

'The Excavations at Carthage' (29 May 1858, p. 545).

1859

'The Arrival of the Remains of the Tomb of Mausolus at the British Museum' (22 January 1859, pp. 83 and 85).

'The Ruins of Carthage' (12 March 1859, p. 251).

1861

'Sculptures from Halicarnassus and Cnidus' (19 October 1861, pp. 401 and 403).

'The Cyrene Marbles in the British Museum' (30 November 1861, pp. 563–4).

1873

'The Temple at Ephesus' (22 March 1873, p. 282).

'Nineveh and its Records' (15 November 1857, n.p.).

1875

'The Ruins of Ephesus' (3 April 1875, p. 329).

1876

'The Ruins of Ephesus' (16 November 1876, p. 473).

1878

'Recent Assyrian Discoveries by Mr. Rassam' (16 November 1878, pp. 464–6).

1883

'Babylonian Antiquities at the British Museum' (17 March 1883, p. 277).

1884
'Assyrian and Babylonian Relics at the British Museum' (19 January 1884, pp. 67 and 72).

1887
'Hittite Inscriptions' (26 March 1887, pp. 347 and 349).

1888
'Antiquities of Tenedos' (8 December 1888, p. 671).

1889
'Egyptian Antiquities in the British Museum' (29 December 1889, p. 831).

Appendix 4:
HMS *Caledonia*: extract from log book, 1872[1]

1872
Moored in Smyrna Harbour
10 January – Employed hoisting in marbles from Ephesus.
Received 26 cases and one marble block.

24 January – Employed hoisting in marbles from Ephesus.
Received 7 cases containing marble & one block.

25 January – a.m. Employed hoisting in marbles from Ephesus.
– p.m. – Received three blocks of marble.

29 January – Received 4 blocks & 2 cases of marble.

30 January – a.m. Received 5 cases of marble.
– p.m. Employed hoisting in marbles from Ephesus …
received 10 cases of marble.

31 January – Received 8 cases of marble from Ephesus.

At Malta
14 February – Employed hoisting out cases of marble.

15 February – a party at Dockyard landing marbles from
Ephesus.

Total – fifty-eight cases of marble and nine blocks of marble.

---

[1] TNA, ADM 53/994.

BIBLIOGRAPHY

Primary Sources

National Archives, Public Record Office, Kew London (TNA)
Admiralty papers

Foreign Office papers

Treasury papers

Colonial Office papers

British Museum
Collection Online: https://www.britishmuseum.org/research/
collection_online/search.aspx

Newspapers and magazines
Aberdeen Weekly Journal

Birmingham Daily Post

The Gentleman's Magazine

The Graphic

The Guardian

Illustrated Berwick Journal

The Illustrated London News

The Malta Times

Morning Chronicle

The Saturday Review

The Times

Parliamentary documents

An Act to vest the Elgin Collection of ancient Marbles and
    Sculpture in the Trustees of the British Museum for the
    Use of the Public (1816). Public Act, 56 George III, c.
    99. <http://discovery.nationalarchives.gov.uk/details/
    rd/647d80ec-79a1-4cca-8383-2302cbf08c63>.

Historic Hansard (1803–2005). <http://hansard.
    millbanksystems.com/commons/>. (House of
    Commons and House of Lords debates.)

Parliamentary Archives. Houses of Parliament, London.
    <http://www.parliament.uk/business/publications/
    parliamentary-archives/>

ProQuest UK Parliamentary Papers (UK PP). <http://
    parlipapers.proquest.com/parlipapers>. (Institution/
    library subscription required).

The Holocaust (Return of Cultural Objects) Act 2009
    <https://services.parliament.uk/Bills/2017-19/
    holocaustreturnofculturalobjectsamendment.html>.

The Human Tissue Act 2004 <https://www.legislation.gov.uk/
    ukpga/2004/30/contents>.

Secondary sources

A Guide to the Exhibition galleries of the British Museum, Bloomsbury.
    London: Printed By order of the Trustees, 1888.

Aitchison, George. 'The Temple of Diana at Ephesus', *The
    Times*, 24 April 1890, p. 12.

Alberge, Dalya. 'Turkey turns to human rights law to reclaim
    British Museum sculptures', *The Guardian*, 8 December
    2012 <www.theguardian.com/culture/2012/dec/08/
    turkey-british-museum-eculptures 16/03/2016>.

Allgood, George. *China War 1860 Letters and Journal.* London:
    Longmans & Co., 1901.

Antiquities of Ionia published by The Society of Dilettanti. London:
    W. Bulmer, 1821.

Barnett, Richard D. et al. *Sculptures from the Southwest Palace of
    Sennacherib at Nineveh.* London: British Museum Press,
    1998.

Beechey, Captain F.W. et al. *Proceedings of the Expedition to explore the Northern Coast of Africa, from Tripoli eastward; in 1821 and 1822.* London: John Murray, 1828.

Bennett, Terry. *History of Photography in China 1842–1860.* London: Quaritch, 2009.

Brusius, Mirjam. 'Photography's Fits and Starts: The Search for Antiquity and its Image in Victorian Britain', *History of Photography*, vol. 40 (London: Routledge, 2016), pp. 250–66.

Bürger, W. *Trésors d'art en Angleterre.* Bruxelles and Ostende: Librairie de Ferdinand Claassen, 1860.

Carter, Joseph Coleman. *The Sculpture of the Sanctuary of Athena Polias.* London: The Society of Antiquaries of London with British Museum Publications, 1983.

Challis, Debbie. *From the Harpy Tomb to the Wonders of Ephesus.* London: Duckworth, 2008.

Cima, Keith H. *Reflections from the Bridge.* Whittlebury: Baron, 1994.

Classified List of Photographs of Works of Decorative Art in the Victoria and Albert Museum, and other Collections. London: HMSO, 1901.

Cobain, Ian. *The History Thieves.* London: Portobello, 2016.

Cust, Lionel. *History of the Society of Dilettanti.* Reissued with supplementary chapter, etc. London: Macmillan, 1914.

Davis, Dr N. *Carthage and her Remains: Being an account of the excavations and researches on the site of the Phoenician metropolis conducted under the Auspices of Her Majesty's Government.* London: Richard Bentley, 1861.

Dennis, George. *The Cities and Cemeteries of Etruria.* 2 vols. London: John Murray, 1848; rev. ed., 1878.

Edwards, Edward. *Lives of The Founders of the British Museum; with notices of its chief augmentors and other benefactors 1570–1870.* London: Trübner, 1870.

Fellows, Charles. *A Journal written during an excursion in Asia Minor.* London: John Murray, 1839.

Fellows, Charles. *Narrative of an Ascent to the Summit of Mount Blanc of the 25 July 1827*. London: printed by Thomas Davidson, 1827.

Fellows, Charles. *The Xanthian Marbles: their Acquisition, and Transmission to England*. London: John Murray, 1843.

Franks, Augustus W. *On Recent Excavations and Discoveries on the Site of Ancient Carthage*. London: J. B. Nichols and Sons, 1860.

Gadd, C.J. *The Stones of Assyria*. London: Chatto & Windus, 1936.

Goodchild, J.E. *A Study of the Marbles from Ephesus in the British Museum. With suggestions on the restoration of the temple of Diana, as shewn in Mr. J.T. Wood's 'Discoveries at Ephesus'*. Walthamstow: printed for private circulation, 1889.

Gunning, Lucia Patrizio. *The British Consular Service in the Aegean and the Collection of Antiquities for the British Museum*. Farnham: Ashgate, 2009.

Harris, David. *Of Battle and Beauty: Felice Beato's Photographs of China*. Santa Barbara: Santa Barbara Museum of Art, 1999.

Hicks, E. L. 'Judith and Holofernes', *The Journal of Hellenic Studies*, vol. 6 (1885), pp. 261–94.

Higgins, Charlotte. 'Director of the British Museum, Hartwig Fisher, reveals plans for an extensive revamp, but won't be drawn on calls to return plundered works', *The Guardian*, 14 April 2018, pp. 6–7.

Holmes, Richard Rivington. *Naval and Military Trophies & Personal Relics of British Heroes*. London: John C. Nimmo, 1896.

Howe, Kathleen Stewart. *Revealing the Holy Land: The Photographic Exploration of Palestine*. Reviewed by Peter Clark in *British Journal of Middle Eastern Studies*, vol. 25, no. 2 (1998): 303–304.

Inscriptions in the Phoenician Character now deposited in the British Museum discovered on the site of Carthage, during researches made by Nathan Davis Esq., at the expense of her Majesty's Government in the years 1856, 1857 and 1858. London: printed by order of the Trustees, 1863.

Ionian Antiquities, published by order of The Society of Dilettanti.
London: printed by T. Spilsbury and W. Haskell, 1769.

Jenkins, Ian. *Archaeologists & Aesthetes in the Sculpture Galleries of
the British Museum 1800–1939.* London: British Museum
Press, 1992.

Jenkins, Ian. *Greek Architecture and Its Sculpture in the British
Museum.* London: The British Museum Press, 2006.

Jenkins, Tiffany. *Keeping their Marbles: how the treasures of the
past ended up in museums ... and why they should stay there.*
Oxford: Oxford University Press, 2016.

Kennedy, Maeve. 'British Museum cracks case of looted Iraqi
art', *The Guardian,* 9 August 2018, p. 19.

Layard, Austen Henry. *Discoveries in the ruins of Nineveh and
Babylon: with travels in Armenia, Kurdistan and the desert:
being the result of a second expedition undertaken for the
Trustees of the British Museum.* 2 vols. London: John
Murray, 1853.

Layard, Austen Henry. *A Popular Account of Discoveries at
Nineveh.* London, 1851.

Layard, Austen Henry. *Nineveh and Its Remains.* 2 vols. London:
John Murray, 1849.

Lewis, O.M. *China's Summer Palace: Finding the Missing Imperial
Treasures.* London: High Tile Books, 2017.

Lewis, O.M. *The Mortgage on the Elgin Marbles.* London: High
Tile Books, 2016.

*List of Objects in the Art Division South Kensington Museum,
Lent during the Year 1872.* London: George E. Eyre and
William Spottiswood, 1873.

Loch, Henry Brougham (Lord Loch). *Personal Narrative of
Occurrences During Lord Elgin's Second Embassy to China in
1860.* London: John Murray, 1900.

MacGregor, Neil. Preface to *Enlightenment: Discovering the World
in the Eighteenth Century.* Eds Kim Sloan with Andrew
Burnett. London: British Museum Press, 2003.

Macintyre, Ben. 'Archive at "spook central" had secret Mau
Mau files', *The Times,* 8 April 2011, p. 10.

Macintyre, Ben. 'Embarrassing colonial files hidden for years were Foreign Office's "guilty secret"', *The Times*, 6 May 2011, p. 20.

Marriott, James. 'How Britain's cultural jewels were saved from the Blitz', *The Times*, 2 July 2019, pp. 8–9.

Marshall, F.H. *Catalogue of the Jewellery, Greek Etruscan and Roman in the Department of Antiquities, British Museum.* First published 1911. Oxford: Oxford University Press, 1969.

Meyer, Karl E. *The Plundered Past: The Traffic in Art Treasures.* London: Penguin, 1973.

Murray, A.S., A.H. Smith and H.B. Walters, *Excavations in Cyprus.* Bequest of Miss E. T. Turner to the British Museum. London: The Trustees of the British Museum, 1900.

Murray, A.S. *Terracotta Sarcophagus: Greek and Etruscan in the British Museum.* London: Longmans, 1898.

Newton, C.T. 'Recent Acquisitions in the Department of Greek and Roman Antiquities at the British Museum', *The Fine Arts Quarterly Review*, vol. 1 (May 1863), pp. 191–2.

Newton, C.T. *A History of Discoveries at Halicarnassus, Cnidus and Branchidae Being the Results of an Expedition sent to Asia Minor by H.M. Government in 1856. Assisted by R.P. Pullan, Esq. F.R.I.B.A.* 2 vols. London: Day and Son, 1862.

Newton, C.T. ed. *The Collection of Ancient Greek Inscriptions in the British Museum* 4 vols. Oxford: The Clarendon Press, 1874–1916.

Newton, C.T. *Travels and Discoveries in the Levant.* 2 vols. London: Day & Sons, 1865.

Ohnefalsch-Richter, Max. *Kypros: The Bible and Homer.* London: Asher & Co. 1893.

Oxford Dictionary of National Biography (ODNB) <http://www.oxforddnb.com>.

Porter, Major-General Whitworth. *The History of the Corps of Royal Engineers.* London: Longmans, 1889.

Rassam, Hormuzd *Asshur and the Land of Nimroud: being an account of the discoveries made in the ancient ruins of Nineveh, Asshur, Sepharvaim, Calah, Babylon, Borsippa, Cuthah and Van.* New York: Eaton & Mains, 1897.

Rassam, Hormuzd. 'Letter to the Editor', *The Times*, 5 April 1894, p. 14.

Rawlinson, George. *A Memoire of Major-General Sir Henry Creswicke Rawlinson.* London: Longmans, Green, and Co., 1898.

Rawlinson, H. C. *A Selection from the Historical Inscriptions of Chaldaea, Assyria and Babylonia.* 5 vols. London: Lithographed by R. E. Bowler, 1861.

Sage, Adam. 'Louvre unveils Euro 1bn Abu Dhabi outpost', *The Times*, 7 September 2007, p. 37.

Sanderson David and Adam Sage. 'Britain sends treasures back to Africa', *The Times*, 22 November 2018, p. 3.

Sanderson, David. 'British Museum cracks cold case of Sumerian treasures looted from Iraq', *The Times*, 10 August 2018, p. 20.

Smith, A. H. *A Catalogue of Sculpture in the Department of Greek and Roman Antiquities, British Museum.* 3 vols. London: Longmans, 1904.

Smith, A. H. *The Mausoleum and Sculptures of Halicarnassus and Priene in the British Museum.* London: printed by order of the trustees of the British Museum, 1900.

Smith, Robert Murdoch, R.E., and Edwin Augustus Porcher, R.N. *History of the Recent Discoveries at Cyrene made during an Expedition to the Cyrenaica in 1860–61, under the Auspices of Her Majesty's Government.* London: Day, 1864.

Sotheby, S. Leigh and John Williams. 'Ancient Greek Pottery excavated by Messrs. Biliotti & Salzmann, in the necropolis of Camirus, Island of Rhodes', Lugt number 26784. Catalogue. 10 May 1862.

Synopsis of the Contents of the British Museum: Department of Greek and Roman Antiquities: Greco-Roman Sculptures. 2 vols. London: Printed by Order of the Trustees, 1874–6.

The British Museum, Fact sheet (2015) <https://www.britishmuseum.org/pdf/fact_sheet_bm_collection.pdf>.

The British Imperial Calendar. London: Varnham, 1860.

The Foreign Office List. London: Harrison and Sons, 1869 and 1898.

The Navy List. London: John Murray, 1839–91

Thompson, E. Maunde. 'Mr. Rassam', *The Times*, 29 July 1892, p. 6.

Waterfield, Gordon. *Layard of Nineveh*. London: London: John Murray, 1963.

Wilson, David M. *The British Museum: A History*. London: The British Museum Press, 2002.

Wood, J. T. *Discoveries at Ephesus, including the site and remains of the Great Temple of Diana*. London: Longmans, Green, and Co., 1877.

Wright, William. *List of the Magdala Collection of Ethiopic Manuscripts in the British Museum*. Leipzig: Deutsche Morgenländische Gessellschaft, 1875.

INDEX

A

Abu Dhabi 166

Abyssinia 164; photographs at 156–8

Acheron, HMS 21

Admiralty 4, 7, 9, 11, 15, 16–17, 19–29, 163, 169–71; Assyria & Babylon 62; Carthage 92–3; Cyrene 82, 83, 85; Ephesus 67, 70–1, 72; Halicarnassus, Cnidus & Branchidae 38, 41, 42, 43, 146; Mount Aaron 130; Priene 45, 46, 47, 48, 49, 53; Rhodes & Bodrum 76–7; Sicily, North Africa & Turkey 109; Xanthus 99, 100, 101. *See also* HM Ships *and individual ship names*

Adventure, HMS 25

Africa. *See* North Africa

Agincourt, HMS 14, 21

Alexandria 14, 19, 155

Algiers, HMS 21

Amphion, HMS 14, 21

Antelope, HMS 21, 47, 48, 71, 72

Apollo, HMS 21

Apollo, Temple of (Branchidae) 34, 35, 39, 53, 148

Apprentice (merchant ship) 62

archaeologists 1, 2, 4, 10, 35, 52, 54, 57, 74, 86, 109, 118, 122, 167

Ariadne, HMS 71, 72

Artemis, Temple of. *See* Diana, Temple of

Asia Minor 34, 41, 60, 103, 108, 136, 143

Assurance, HMS 21, 83

Assyria 1, 2, 3, 4, 5, 8, 9, 11, 19, 26, 27, 57–66, 90, 122–6, 135, 137, 141, 146, 161, 164; photographs at 144–5

Athena Polias, Temple of (Priene) 11, 28, 45–55, 137, 153, 164

Athens 19, 137

B

C

Also by O. M. Lewis and
published by High Tile Books

China's Art for Arms
Finding the Missing Imperial Treasures
ISBN 978-0-9954953-1-9 (paperback)
ISBN 978-0-9954953-0-2 (ebook)

China's Summer Palace
Finding the Missing Imperial Treasures
ISBN 978-0-9954953-4-0 (paperback)

China's Lost Art Loan
Finding the Missing Imperial Treasures
ISBN 978-0-9954953-5-7 (paperback)

The Mortgage on the Elgin Marbles
ISBN 978-0-9954953-3-3 (paperback)
ISBN 978-0-9954953-2-6 (ebook)

Available from all good book shops
or on Amazon